SCIENCE, NATURE AND IDENTITY

Understanding the Value
of Experiential Learning
in a Land Art Context

SCIENCE, NATURE AND IDENTITY

Understanding the Value of Experiential Learning in a Land Art Context

LUCY MEDHURST

STOUR**VALLEY** ARTS

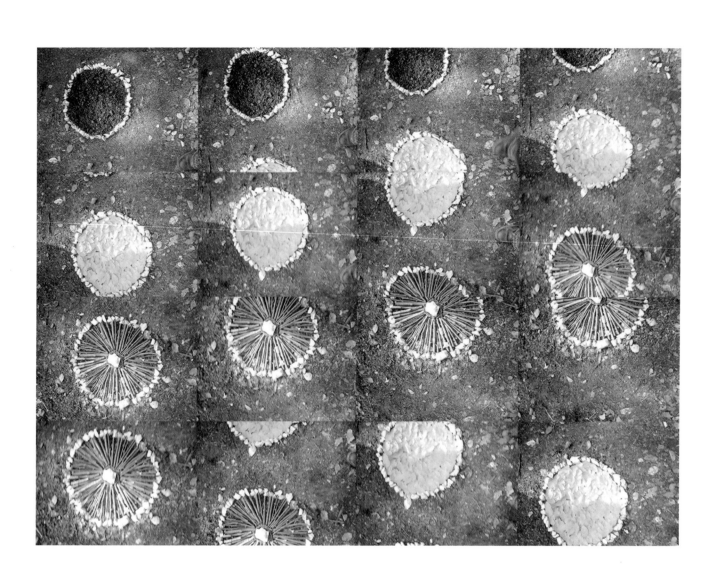

CONTENT

PLEASE CHECK FOR 2 DISCS IN BACK OF BOOK

CHAPTER FIVE

Susan Derges, *Repository No2*, 1999

CHAPTER ONE

Introduction
SVA Case Study
Research Methodology

INTRODUCTION

The topic of this dissertation builds on the short term paper *Ecologies of Practice, Outdoor Learning and the Arts* and will look at the field in more depth. The key question of the research is to examine what educational outcomes emerge through using experiential learning in a Land Art context, to define the context and the learning methodology in order to identify the value of this approach. The literature review considers current research in education to define what is meant by the term "experiential learning". Reference will be made to relevant literature and theory from the fields of neuroscience, education, psychology and environmental psychology, but it is not within the scope of this dissertation to conduct an exhaustive review of education literature.

Chapter Three will look at distilling the theories into learning outcomes, using studies from existing research of long term practice such as Forest Schools (FS), Creative Partnerships (CP) and other relevant primary research and reports. This chapter will attempt to map the outcomes onto the research in order to inform the research methodology for the primary research material.

The research poses questions about perceptions of risk and whether traditionally this kind of learning has been more accessible to particular groups. Issues of gender, social background, disaffection and medical diagnosis (of conditions such as Attention Deficit Hyperactivity Disorder (ADHD)) will be examined in relation to the topic in order to discover whether there may be a particular value for certain groups offered by this kind of learning. The themes of well-being and of learning disengagement will be addressed, particularly because they are central elements in the 'Down Time' project, funded through the health authority and the

National Lottery. Evidence from the case studies and interviews will be used to answer the question about the value of this practice as well as any challenges, unexpected findings and counter-arguments.

Finally, some conclusions may be reached and gaps identified for further research.

SVA CASE STUDY

SVA provides a unique context in which to work and further description is warranted to set the scene for the themes of this paper. The organisation was the subject of an earlier paper *"Survival of the Fittest: small organisations and change"* which described how the organisation was founded in direct response to Grizedale, another Forestry Commission (FC) site with commissioned work (Medhurst 2009 p.4). Like Grizedale, SVA is based on 1500 acres of FC land, in a designated Area of Outstanding Natural Beauty (AONB) at King's Wood, Challock, Kent whereas Grizedale is a much larger site at 6046 acres and incorporates many of the facilities and visitor attractions of other FC sites.[1] Although both are working forest sites, King's Wood is unique in having no visitor centre or other attractions, apart from the on site artworks and events commissioned by SVA. Originally the Grizedale commissions were based on *"artists' residences which last up to six months"......" Some sculpture is of a temporary nature whilst other work is more permanent"* (Grant and Harris 1991 p.19). Defining themselves firmly as *"not a Sculpture Park"* Grizedale acknowledged affinities with *"environmental and green campaigning (art) groups, most notably Common Ground"* but with the difference of not being rooted in community art but allowing artists to make *"an individual(s) response to a particular landscape, a large production forest"* (p.19). SVA's Director Sandra Drew set the mission as *"a unique project, which aims to increase public awareness of contemporary art while encouraging greater interest in the environment".*[2] This uniqueness lies in a deep engagement with the originally undeveloped 1500 acre site in line with the her vision: *"The notion of commissioning site-specifically, of supporting artists work in progress and of giving artists a long time to develop a proposal was what interested me from the beginning. I wanted to support artists to really engage with the place, to not have to hurry the artistic and curatorial process"* (Drew and Kent 2005 p.69). Indeed the first commission to Richard Harris *Untitled* 1994 involved works in two old flint pits that have now all but vanished back into the forest floor. His other growing piece *Untitled* took seven years to come to fruition and be declared to the public (Drew and Kent p.89). Site specific has included work that is physically sited at King's Wood with great sensitivity to the environment

1 In the South East an examples are Bedgebury Pinetum and in the South West CCANW. Both have Go Ape, cycle hire, visitor centre, café and extensive parking.

2 Mission statement Drew 2007

and work that may be time-based, performative or ephemeral, created as a response. There have been films, publications and exhibitions complementing and extending the on-site commissions.

SVA has included education since its inception. In the words of the Director: *"We have always considered that our education programme is an essential part of our long term audience development strategy....it has always been fundamental to what SVA does"* (Drew & Kent 2005 p.76). The education and learning strand of SVA's work has evolved beyond the aim of audience development alone. The long-term in depth nature of the artists' commissions feeds and is reflected in the education and learning programmes, and this has been consciously pursued, particularly in recent years, with the aim of deepening and extending the learning experience over longer periods of time, allowing new and exciting material to be generated and used as a continuously refreshed and changing resource:
" I was talking to a teacher who ...is teaching science around chlorophyll and was so excited to have the opportunity to see Edwina Fitzpatrick's texts about her chlorophyll experiments: a good example of the commissioned work feeding back into education" (op. cit p.77)[3]

The education and learning programme trains and employs freelance artists and ecologists to work with the King's Wood site and to help devise and deliver projects, which engage with all aspects of the site and the artistic commissions. This can involve history, geography, geology, ecology and science, directly experienced through the site and a range of themes related to the commissions themselves. In 2010 'Vibration Station' was a sound project with 72 primary school children, alongside the residency of sound artist Lee Patterson and resulting in a combined exhibition. In 2007, a proposal made by Canterbury College student Christopher Jones became a temporary installation 'Forest Stars', based on his research into the power generating properties of decomposing pine needles. In itself this commission provided a curatorial learning experience for a new and emerging artist. SVA's diversity is a strength but also a potential weakness in that there is no single fixed pedagogy or learning programme that is being delivered over time, as in the case of FS, apart from one-off walks and one day workshops. Neither does SVA follow programming timetables tied in to exhibitions as galleries do, however the consistent theme is the site, contemporary art practice and environmental and ecological concerns. Consistent too is an approach that focuses on learning both through the site, through art and over time.

Due to the nature of contemporary art practice and a continuously evolving debate that surrounds it, the learning programme at SVA needs

3 This may result in specific year-long projects like 'From The Ground Up' 'Exploring the Context' and 'Art<>Eco' but also means that there is always new material being generated around new commissions. The Enquire programme, funded by Engage and in collaboration with Turner Contemporary and Canterbury Museums Service has resulted in a series of downloadable themed resources like *Maths Through Pattern* 2009, which have been extremely popular. Downloads continue at the rate of 2000+ per annum.

14

to be responsive and creative. Not all projects are exclusively delivered at the King's Wood site but there is a strong emphasis on bringing children young people and groups to experience the natural environment and the changing seasons. This gives SVA a rich variety of learning possibilities to draw from, including the Neolithic remains and the continuing research undertaken by different artists. The aim is to create a learning community mutually benefiting from one another's experiences and insights. SVA also works with other partners in Kent, UK and internationally to strengthen its cultural offer. It should also be stated that the learning programme has no dedicated core budget but relies on funding applications to support its long-term projects. It operates in a rural context, seven miles from Ashford, the nearest urban centre.

RESEARCH METHODOLOGY

Using a research framework and grounded analysis theory, Stour Valley Arts (SVA) primary research on the Down Time project will be studied, including film, action research journals and evaluations. Phase 1 included training followed by supported practice with the different participant groups. The Field Notes Guide provided the thematic research lens and was shared with the teachers, social and care workers and the artists involved in phase 2 of Down Time.[4] The arguments, theory and question will be tested through a series of interviews with artists, practitioners and teachers with relevant experience of FS, CP and SVA. The questions have been formulated in order to explore how different practitioners view the work of SVA and of parallel cultural organisations to examine differences and similarities in experience and learning. The journals include drawings, ideas, mind maps and recorded conversations and thoughts made during the project and beyond. Permissions were sought from all participants to be photographed recorded and for materials to be part of the research. In order to protect the identities of those involved, no actual names are used and interviewees are identified in terms of their profession and experience only.[5] As broad a range of individuals as possible were consulted and every effort has been made to avoid bias.

4 See Appendix 1

5 See Appendix 7 and Figure 3 p.70

CHAPTER TWO

LITERATURE REVIEW

This review will examine the literature and theories relevant to the critical context for this dissertation. These will be explored thematically through sub topics as follows:

- Learning theories and experiential learning
- Neuroscience, environmental psychology and psychology
- Well-being agenda
- Art education (in particular relating to galleries and museums)

In the short term paper, several works were reviewed and analysed, especially the Review of Research on Outdoor Learning (RROL) (2004) as well as the literature on learning in galleries and museums and evaluation frameworks used (Medhurst 2008 pp.4 – 10). The RROL was commissioned to look at available research on outdoor learning in different contexts and was the research base for the Learning Outside the Classroom (LOTC) manifesto, launched in 2006. The RROL acknowledged a movement towards more qualitative and process based approaches but failed to take advantage of existing evaluation frameworks from the cultural sector such as the Generic Learning Outcomes (GLOs) used by museums. Pringle's contemporary gallery education (CGE) framework came out of a review commissioned by the Arts Council (ACE), also in 2006. Pringle looked at international evaluation models, critiqued them and devised her own framework which was designed to be suitable for learning specifically within the context of contemporary art practice and galleries or museums whose learning programmes had this focus. This dissertation takes the previous paper as its departure point and has evolved from prior reading and research. It will examine art education in more depth following consideration of the other sub topics listed above.

BACKGROUND

An attempt to unravel the origins of the current dichotomy between mainstream education and the philosophies of experiential learning, leads the researcher into labyrinthine paths. Important thinkers such as Dewey, Read, Piaget and Vygotsky and their theories have shaped and informed current practice, but it is a topic that is under continued debate, interpretation and re-evaluation. Alongside this, educational policy also exerts influence as the tension between policy-led instrumental and alternative approaches demonstrates. The current debate over Standard Attainment Tests (SATS) is a case in point. Long upheld as the evidential base to prove the efficacy of current teaching practice, it is now criticised for causing undue stress to teachers and pupils and of being *"misused to compile meaningless league tables, which only serve to humiliate and demean children"* (http://news.bbc. co.uk/1/hi/education/8635017.stm). Neither is the apparent dichotomy a clearly defined one. There is acknowledgement, both from Ofsted in respect of art teaching and learning and recognised to some extent in initiatives like the Outdoor Learning Manifesto (OLM) and the RROL that experiential learning may have something to offer (Medhurst, 2009 pp.2-4). It is arguable that the evidence and theoretical underpinning for this are still lacking, or rather, their intrinsic process-oriented and qualitative nature is critiqued by and at odds with a culture in education in the UK that still requires standardised methods of comparison and measurement. This standardisation has it roots in the original, corrective view of education *"which, in the old and literal sense of the word, prevents us in the ways of evil"* (Read 1964 p.6). Anna Cutler writes that *"education is ideologically driven"* meaning *"the dominant, hegemonically maintained hierarchy of value"* (2010, p.2). Much good has been achieved by continuous assessment but unfortunately: *"The current system seems to reward teachers who can teach to get children through national tests. Good test results seem to have become an end in themselves. Not just a measure of achievement but the system's goal"* (Leadbetter 2008, p.17). An unfortunate corollary to this is that this transmission style teaching and focus on tests results *"may particularly disadvantage those children most likely to be turned off by academic subjects and traditional teaching "* (ibid). In spite of a raft of research in cultural organisations and many innovative pilots into changing the way that schools are structured and work in their communities, change is slow and subject to the vagaries of education policy.[6]

6 See Leadbetter *'What's Next? 21 Ideas for 21st Century Learning'* (2008)

PIONEERS

The origins of experiential education have their roots in the writings of John Dewey, an American philosopher who wrote 'How We Think. A restatement of the relation of reflective thinking to the educative process' 1933, 'Art as Experience' 1934 and 'Experience and Education' in 1938. Dewey explored the tension between traditional approaches and " the fundamental unity of the newer philosophy" defining the latter as " the idea that there is an intimate and necessary relation between the processes of actual experience and education. [Dewey, 1938,pp.19,20] (Kolb 1984 p.5). It is important to note that he had an understanding of artistic process as a means to learning and his influence also extends to the field of outdoor learning and higher education. Equally his philosophy did not lack rigour: "The belief that all genuine education comes from experience does not mean that all experiences are genuinely or equally educative. Experience and education cannot be directly equated to each other" (1938, p.25). He debated the issues posed by the "new education" and the role of the teacher:
"The teacher's suggestion is not a mold for a cast-iron result but is a starting point to be developed into a plan through contributions from the experience of all engaged in the learning process" (Dewey,1938, p.72). His democratic view of engagement and his identification of learning as a process are critical. We shall see how his views have been taken up and influenced later Constructivist theory.

Dewey's philosophy and his pragmatic approach, offered an alternative to the Behaviourist theories of B.F. Skinner (1904 – 1999) and Ivan Pavlov (1849 – 1936). Pavlov was a Russian psychologist and physician who famously conducted experiments with dogs. Pavlov observed reflex responses to stimuli and this led to the theory of classical conditioning, as interpreted in the West, following publication of Pavlov's ideas in 1927 (Bigge and Shermis, 2004 pp.79-80). Skinner's experiments led him to believe that learning was the acquisition of new (required) behaviour by use of reward (positive reinforcement) or punishment (disapproval):

"Such behaviours are inculcated by adults telling, showing, directing, guiding, arranging, manipulating, rewarding, punishing, and, at times, coercing the activities of children and youth. Accordingly, teaching is a matter of adults setting behavioristic environmental conditions – stimuli – to ensure that students accomplish educational goals"
(Bigge and Shermis, 2004 p.78).

Pedagogic instruction and curriculum-based measurement models, which are elements of mainstream education today, can be seen to derive from this model. However, Skinner also opposed corporal punishment and had an interest in the environment, which he believed helped shape behaviour. The environmental movement owes a great deal to Henri David Thoreau who wrote *Walden: Life in the Woods* published in 1854. Skinner wrote a novel called *Walden II*, published in 1948 in which he described a utopian society living in nature, controlled and shaped as if in a laboratory by *"cultural engineering"* (Kolb, 1984 p.34). This alarming vision was discredited partly because of its popularity among fascists.

Kurt Lewin (1890 – 1947) was a psychologist who developed a system acknowledging *"that a human being is a complex biological organism in a cultural or social environment"* which was the root of Cognitivism. Lewin developed the concept of "life space" that is essentially a holistic view of the individual (Bigge & Shermis, 2004, p.180). There is an individuated sense of meaning construction. This was then developed with Dewey's theories of education into a personal meaning making derived from experience, which then motivates and develops the learner (ibid p.181). These early pioneers were the forerunners of Cognitive-Field Interactionist Learning Theory. There is a clear difference between the behaviorists with their Stimulus Response Conditioning Theories and the Cognitivists who were more concerned with an approach which made sense of the individual experience as part of a social and cultural context rather than instructing and instilling in set and fixed perameters.

Herbert Read (1893–1968) was an admirer and critic of Dewey. He was an anarchist poet, co-founder of the Institute of Contemporary Arts (ICA) with Roland Penrose, and editor of the Burlington Magazine. Read was influential in many spheres and was knighted by Winston Churchill. His seminal work *"Education Through Art"* published in 1943, involves an in-depth comprehensive analysis of educational theories, from Plato onwards. He was also perhaps the first to incorporate psychology, education theory, therapy, philosophy and aesthetics in what was the most detailed investigation into the topic analysing the drawings and paintings of children to prove his thesis. He was a passionate advocate for specialist art teaching. He was critical of Dewey and others for failing to establish a methodology for creative education based in fact:
" It is my belief that their failure to convince the world at large – a world which demands quantitative results, in marks and certificates, rather than a lighting up of the chambers of the imagination, is due to their neglect of **a priori** *considerations. These pioneers have proceeded experimentally and intuitively: some of them, Dewey in particular, have erected a pragmatic philosophy on the results of their experience; but they have not sought the basis of a method, as Rousseau did, in the objective facts of human nature."*
He was critical of much of contemporary education, too: *"learning is often* **knowing** *without much care for* **feeling** *and mostly none at all for*

doing" (Read, 1964, p.231). Like many writers and thinkers of this period, he had a radical vision of culture: *"Every man is a special kind of artist, and in his originating activity, his play or work....he is doing more than express himself: he is manifesting the form which our common life should take, in its unfolding"* (op.cit.p.308). The social and cultural dimensions of education were central to his philosophy and he was a passionate advocate for the importance of art (or aesthetic) education and creativity to a healthy society:

"The world influences the child as nature and as society. The elements educate him —air, light, the life of plants and animals; and relationships educate him. The true educator comprises both; but he must be to the child as one of the elements" (Read 1964, p.288).

The problem for education systems has been to integrate a holistic aesthetic approach with the requirements of a curriculum that sets fixed content and measures of progression. Read was ahead of his time and his arguments are still unresolved today.

Another very important figure was Lev Vygotsky (1896 –1934) a Russian psychologist who lived during the Revolution. His major work was largely unknown to the West until *"Thought and Language"* was translated into English in the 1960s (Bigge & Shermis, 2004 p.124). Vygotsky's theory of learning involved the concept of zones of proximal development or ZPDs, *"the role of education was to provide children with experiences that were within their ZPDs...The teacher's task is to keep each child's learning tasks either centred on, or focused slightly above each respective child's ZPD"* (Bigge and Shermis p.129). He also acknowledged the importance of play especially to the Early Years (Bigge and Shermis p.131).

Vygotsky's importance was recognised by David Kolb in his seminal work *"Experiential Learning: Experience as the Source of Learning and Development"* published in 1984. His book acknowledges the *"origins of experiential learning in the works of John Dewey, Kurt Lewin and Jean Piaget.....and proposes a model of the underlying structure of the learning process based on research in psychology, philosophy and physiology"* (1984 p.xi). Acknowledging that *"we are the learning species, and our survival depends on our ability to adapt not only in the reactive sense of fitting into the physical and social worlds, but in the proactive sense of creating and shaping those worlds"* (1984 p.1) Kolb demonstrates how Lewin, Dewey and Piaget contributed to contemporary experiential learning theory.[7]

Lewin's ideas led to the development of action research, used in gallery education in the UK today. These ideas *"represent external challenges to... philosophies that have dominated thinking about learning and education since the Middle Ages"* (Kolb 1984 p.12). Jean Piaget, a student of Alfred Binet, who developed the first aptitude and intelligence quotient (IQ)

7 See Fig.1

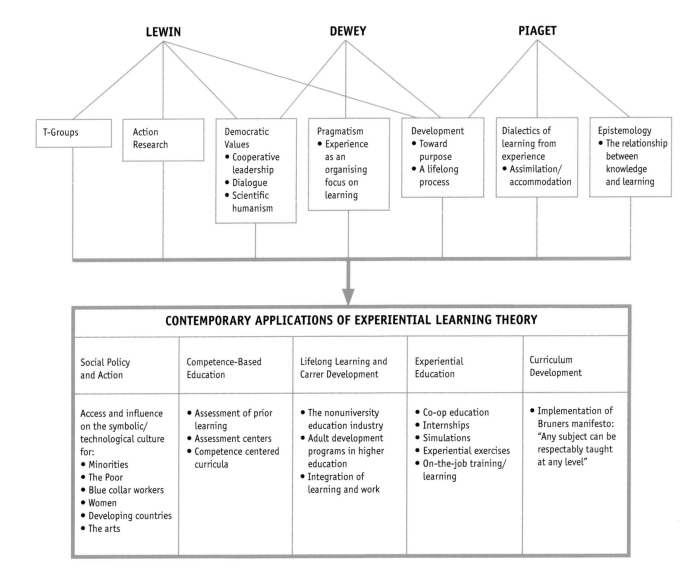

Fig 1. KOLB, DAVID A., EXPERIENTIAL LEARNING: EXPERIENCE AS A SOURCE OF LEARNING
& DEVELOPMENT, 1st Edition ©1984, Figure 1.2 p.17. Reprinted by permission of
Pearson Education, Inc, Upper Saddle River, NJ.

tests, made careful observations of children and teenagers in the early 20th century, demonstrating *"that abstract reasoning and the power to manipulate symbols arose from the infant's actions in exploring and coping with the immediate environment"* (Kolb p.12). Piaget's ideas only gained recognition in education in the 1960s and as a result *"learning became more individualised, concrete and self-directed. Moreover the child was learning about the process of discovering knowledge, not just the content. Children became "little scientists"'*(Kolb p.14). However these democratic models of education were not universally adopted or approved and arguably the same tension between instrumental and process oriented practice persists today. Piaget's theories *"also provoked strong reaction and criticism....Some have blamed the decline in SAT scores on the new math and other self-directed curricula that made learning appear to be fun and lacking in disciplined practice of the basics"* (Kolb p.14).

Kolb developed his own models as an adaptation of Lewin's, and his learning styles theory has become very well known. Naturally, the early thinkers and theorists in this field have also been criticised and their ideas interpreted and further developed, particularly Piaget. His linear theory is very much based on Western type schooling and does not stand up in cross-culture studies (Kolb, 1984 p.133). *"For Piaget, all development is cognitive development. Experiential learning theory describes four development dimensions – affective complexity, perceptual complexity, symbolic complexity and behavioural complexity-all interrelated in the holistic adaptive process of learning"* (Kolb pp.138 – 139). Even then experiential learning has its critics and sceptics who *"see it as gimmicky and faddish, more concerned with technique and process than content and substance"* (Kolb p.3). Australian researcher Brookes makes the case for a rigorous approach and insists that all education has to take into account its social and cultural context in order to be relevant: *"It is not chiselled in granite that outdoor education achieve unique educational benefits, although recognising outdoor education as just one of several alternatives may lend more circumspection to the promotion of outdoor education programs"* (Brookes, 2004, Australian Journal of Outdoor Education, Vol. 8(2), p.22). One of the issues, historically has perhaps been that of a confusion between education, learning and therapeutic benefit, with art not taken seriously as an academic subject and in common with other informal learning contexts, only really considered as viable for those which the mainstream is failing to engage.[8] The argument is more about style and approach than one of quality: difference in technique and process do not of themselves indicate a lack of depth, meaning or substance.

8 See Bentley 1999 2nd ed. pp.90 - 91

CRITIQUES OF EXPERIENTIAL LEARNING AND LEARNING IN THE CLASSROOM

Beard and Wilson look at some of the criticisms of experiential learning, which are broadly summarised as being:

1)   that it lacks direction
2)   that it is subjective and
3)   that Kolb's learning cycle is limited and too simplistic

so that there are:
"critics who argue that there is too great an emphasis on experience to the detriment of the ... curriculum where subjects are taught in traditional and formal classrooms"(2002, p.34).

The issue seems to be that critics see the two as oppositional, identifying an inherent tension between the traditional and formal context and that of experiential learning whose approach is about self-direction and the complexity of learning, which is expressed in many models adapted from Kolb. However Beard and Wilson refer to the *"factory system of learning"* (2002, p.26) in schools or what is referred to in a CP report as *"learned helplessness"* (Galton 2008 p.4). Whitaker articulates this in his *"Managing to Learn, Aspects of Reflective and Experiential Learning in Schools"* when he discusses the problem: *"For many, difficulties in formalized learning in school are created by a deep-seated fear of **getting it wrong,** of being found deficient. For some, there is still the lingering but powerful association between learning and punishment"* (1995 p.11). This is a theme illustrated perfectly by John Holt's book *"How Children Fail"* in which he shares observations from a long teaching career: *"it is meaningless to talk of "succeeding" in playing the cello....There is no line with **Success** written on one side and **Failure** on the other. These words seriously distort our understanding of how we, as well as children, do things and do them better* (1982 p.70). Ultimately what Holt, Whitaker and others argue is that children have a natural desire to learn that is effectively switched off by some schools, which can result in learning disengagement (Whitaker 1995 p.12). Whitaker makes the link between reflective practice and creativity and a dominant *"simplistic and limited model"* of the complexities of teaching and learning, which he feels fails to take research into account (1995 p.25).

In her excellent work *A Handbook of Reflective and Experiential Learning* Jennifer Moon identifies a range of writers, including Csikzentmihalyi who describes a state of "flow" as important in the effective learning process (2004, p.49).[9] She also describes the difference between surface and deep learning as one in which the learner absorbs as much as

9 See also Robinson 2001 p.155.

25

possible for the task in hand contrasted with " *an intention in the learner to understand the material of learning seeking the meaning and understanding the ideas in it"*. She goes on to explain that *"A learner who is interested in a topic is likely to take a deep approach and it appears to be harder for children to sustain this approach when they are anxious or under pressure"* (p.59). Moon engages with the "slipperiness" and "conceptual complexity" of experiential learning (p.106). The author also identifies that: *"One incidental characteristic of experiential learning... is that it is based on theoretical principles that have often been ahead of their time"* (p.112). There is much in common here with other writers referenced in gallery and museum education regarding the constructivist approach to learning, taking into consideration Boud Cohen and Walker's five propositions:

- *Experience is the foundation of, and the stimulus for all learning*
- *Learners actively construct their own experience*
- *Learning is a holistic process*
- *Learning is socially and culturally constructed*
- *Learning is influenced by the socio-emotional context in which it occurs* (2000 pp.8-14 in Moon, 2004 p.111)[10]

Identifying that there is *"some evangelism"* in writings on experiential learning, Moon proposes precisely that this may *"relate to a sense of contrast between 'tedious' classroom learning at which only a few might be seen to excel and learning from life"* but she asks the important question *"Is experiential learning any more effective than formal learning?"* Bringing into the equation important practical considerations about what may be involved *"i.e. has the learner got time to go and sit at the bottom of a volcano for direct experience?"* (p.124). She does however propose that one of the possible 'goods' of experiential learning is its holistic approach, taking the emotion or feeling of the learners into account. Whitaker points out that empathy is a key quality in teachers associated with improved pupil performance (1995 p.108). In addition, Moon highlights the appropriateness of this approach to creative activity: *"Representation of creative and imaginative activity is often based on reflective and experiential learning and in essence, a creative activity involves working with imagination and imagination can be free from already known time and space"* (2004 pp.172 –173).

POLITICS POLICY EMOTIONAL INTELLIGENCE AND NEUROSCIENCE

In discussing instrumental approaches, there is no escaping their origin in politics. Other contributors to the theory of experiential learning are identified by Kolb as Carl Jung[11] and Paolo Freire, a Brazilian educator

26

and revolutionary: *"If it is true that thought has meaning only when generated by action upon the world, the subordination of students to teachers becomes impossible"* (1996 p.58). Freire identified that systems of education which he termed "banking" were more concerned with social control designed to serve and maintain the status quo than with democratic learning. In Kolb's view this was the *'dialectic between the right, which places priority on maintenance of the social order, and the left, which values more highly individual freedom and expression"* (1984 p.16). Kolb also makes claims for the radical nature of experiential learning: *"In the case of social policy and action, experiential learning can be the basis for constructive efforts to promote access to and influence on the dominant technological/symbolic culture for those who have previously been excluded: minorities, the poor, workers, women, people in developing countries, and those in the arts"* (1984 p.18).

It should be remembered, however, that many schools are also pioneering new approaches and are in themselves *"one of the relatively few stable, well-funded and dependable institutions, which operate to a reliable rhythm"* (Leadbetter, 2008 p.31). Many schools work within their communities to provide support and lifelong learning. There are many constraints on schools and on teachers, including having to balance special needs with the needs of the whole class.[12]

In spite of policies like Every Child Matters (2004) and Youth Matters (2005), which aim to focus on the individual learner, policy makers are still grappling with social problems caused by the fallout from learning disengagement.[13] Abraham Maslow's (1908 – 1970) Hierarchy of Needs model underpins much of these policies.[14] Essentially this model deals with individual well-being and human needs. It is *"only when the lower order needs of physical and emotional well-being are satisfied that we are concerned with the higher order needs of influence and personal development"* (www.businessballs.com/maslow.htm). It follows that an individual is unlikely to engage with learning if their basic needs are not met and this is reinforced by recent findings in neuroscience.

Criticising the standard Stanford Binet Intelligence Scale (IQ) test when compared with Gardner's Multiple Intelligence test, for example, Daniel Goleman bemoans adherence to a system which is based *"on a limited notion of intelligence"* (1996 p.38) and one which means: *"we evaluate everyone along the way according to whether they meet that narrow standard of success"* (p.37). Developing an argument for the importance of emotional intelligence in all spheres of life, particularly in terms of social skills, Goleman also points to Leslie Brothers who wrote a seminal paper which *"points to the amygdala and its connections to the association area of the visual cortex as part of the key brain circuitry underlying*

11 Read also references Jung in terms of his theories and how they relate to art (pp.84-6, 96-7, 145-7, 182-93, 204-6).

12 This was referenced by SG when interviewed.

13 For fuller policy overview see (Medhurst, 2008 Short term paper timeline Appendix 1)

14 See Appendix 2

empathy" (p.103). A lack of adequate nurturing and care in infancy can lead to long-term damage and ill health:

"The security of an attachment relationship and the resulting capacity for thinking and reflection facilitated by the caregiver, stimulates development of the more sophisticated parts of the brain, the orbitofrontal cortex. This is involved in complex control and processing mechanisms such as learning, cause and effect thinking, capacity to reflect on behaviour, problem solving, impulse control, as well as emotional resonance and literacy (Enwright 2010 p.1). Such children's capacity to cope in education settings is therefore severely compromised without care and support and frequently leads to behavioural difficulties: *"The healthy integration of the thinking brain and the emotional brain remain unsynchronised resulting in an inability to put the brakes on behavior when in high states of emotional arousal, particularly fear and threat (van der Kolk, 2003; Perry, 1997, 2001, 2005,). Children who have under-developed frontal lobe control as a result of the disorganized attachment, abuse and neglect are therefore more likely to exhibit impulsive behaviour"* (Enwright 2010 p.2).

At Kids Company in their street level centres *"50-60% of the males using the service from age 13 upwards have been excluded from school and prior to engagement with the service were not in education or employment. They have frequently been involved in antisocial behaviour and carry a host of diagnostic labels from the mental health system- many with multiple diagnoses such as ADHD, Autistic Spectrum Disorder (ASD), Conduct Disorder and Oppositional Defiant Disorder (Cook et al 2003, van der Kolk, 2005)"* (Enwright pp.3-4).[15] These young people are falling outside the education training and employment system and without help, are likely to have very limited future prospects:

"The earlier we intervene with these children the swifter and greater the impact the interventions will have on the child's social, emotional and cognitive wellbeing and succeed" (p.7). These findings are supported by research carried out at Harvard University highlighting the importance of training for teachers in dealing with Emotional and Behavioural Difficulty (EBD) to give children the *"social and emotional capabilities that enable them to sit still in a classroom, pay attention, get along with their classmates just as much as they need the cognitive skills required to master the reading and maths concepts"* (Harvard working paper 2, 2004 p.6). The UK comes bottom of the rank for children's well-being in a recent UNICEF study in comparison with North America & 18 European Countries (UNICEF 2007) (NHS 2008 p.3). In the same document the relationship between well-being and issues of educational disengagement including the links between this and mental illness anti-social behaviour and offending. The costs to society are great with the average cost of an individual with untreated conduct disorder estimated at £70,000. [16]

15 Gender and disengagement offers another area of enquiry but attainment is more strongly linked to social background than gender, in spite of international studies which show girls outperforming boys (Croxford Ducklin Frame and Tinklin pp2, 5 and 7) also Ofsted 2003 p.8

16 NIAC 2009 p.5 - for more statistical evidence see pp.6-11

ASSESSMENT CRITERIA AND WELL-BEING

To date, there has not been any fully integrated system for assessing or measuring well-being in the UK. Although not universally used, there is such a model, developed by Ferre Laevers in Belgium in 1976 (2005, p.1). Using the Leuven Involvement Scale for Young Children (LIS-YC scale) *"which provides professionals with a tool for quality assessment of educational settings. It looks at how 'involved' the children are in their work and their 'emotional well-being' allowing (them) to highlight children who may need extra support in the classroom to help each child reach their full potential in terms of learning"* (http://www.kent-eps.org.uk/lpsa2/ summary.pdf). It is used in English Spanish French and German, and with children who have a range of educational needs and is endorsed by the Royal National Institute for the Blind. This system has been piloted in Kent and is relevant to the dissertation because it is in use by some of the settings involved in the primary research.

The Social and Emotional Aspects of Learning (SEAL) curriculum, which seeks to address problems of behaviour and barriers to engagement *"developed as a result of work over the last two years in over 500 schools taking part in the Primary National Strategy's Behaviour and Attendance pilot"*. Its aim is to:
"develop the underpinning qualities and skills that help promote positive behaviour and effective learning. It focuses on five social and emotional aspects of learning: self-awareness, managing feelings, motivation, empathy and social skills"
(http://nationalstrategies.standards.dcsf.gov.uk/primary/publications/ banda/seal) However, this curriculum is for primary level only and is not mandatory, but is intended for schools who have decided to focus on developing these skills in their children.[17] Ofsted's report notes: *"how they have welcomed the more recent materials from the National Strategy, including guidance on effective assessment and monitoring tools. Another barrier to SEAL implementation was resistance expressed by some teachers because they:*
- *anticipated an increase in workload*
- *had reservations about whether this kind of work should be part of their role*
- *thought a focus on social, emotional and behaviour skills would adversely affect academic results"* (www.teachingexpertise.com/ articles/making-secondaryseal-work-2518).

It could be argued that SEAL and Leuven will be implemented only where a school is prepared to invest adequate resources and training. Such intensive observation and record keeping is time consuming and could be criticised for being subjective and open to varying

17 The author knows of one instance at least in Kent where it has been adopted at secondary level

interpretation by teachers and practitioners. The thematic tension between outcomes and outputs as against a more holistic approach, is evidenced in the Ofsted report findings. However, in Manchester the City Council is working with partners to adopt a programme from the USA designed to help children develop emotional resilience. The deputy director of Children's Services estimates that between 30 and 50 percent of the secondary school population would benefit from aspects of this training (Leadbetter, 2008 p.31).

NATURE WRITING AND ENVIRONMENTAL PSYCHOLOGY

Another strand of literature relevant to this dissertation could be categorised as nature writing and environmental psychology. In *"Is Contact with Nature Important for Healthy Child Development? State of the Evidence"* Taylor and Kuo pose the question:
" Is children's need for nature established fact, yet-to-be-substantiated folk theory, or simply myth?" (Spencer & Blades p.120). The relationship between children and their environments is now under enormous pressure and part of the challenge to this relationship lies in perceptions of risk and the freedom to explore, all of which are examined in Richard Louv's book *"Last Child in the Woods: saving our children from nature-deficit disorder"* (2005). Implicit in his argument is the notion of the importance of nature and a sense of one's place in the world as critical to healthy development and individual identity. In an age where electronic media take up an increasing amount of children's time and attention, Louv argues for the therapeutic and cognitive benefits of contact with nature: *" A 2003 survey, published in the journal Psychiatric Services, found the rate at which American children are prescribed antidepressants almost doubled in five years; the steepest increase – 66 percent – was among preschool children"* (p.49). In the U.K. *"In 1993, Hillman reported that the number of unaccompanied activities undertaken by junior age school children at weekends had halved between 1971 and 1990. Arguably this figure continues to fall as local streets and the areas of playgrounds with, for example, fallen trees that have invested meanings are often perceived as areas of risk"* (Whyte, T in Austin, 2007 p.24). At the same time, *"children's access to nature is rapidly diminishing (e.g., Kahn, 2002; Kellert, 2002; Pyle, 2002; Rivkin, 2000)* (Kuo & Taylor in Blades & Spencer p.124). Whilst the authors are sceptical about the effects of the environment per se in achieving particular educational outcomes, other writers point to the fact that *"Interaction with the immediate environment is important for children's emotional well-being and educational development"*, especially in the Early Years, in constructing personal geographies that relate to favourite places (Whyte in Austin, 2007 p.23).

The latest research also points to other indications about direct experience of the environment. Should we be concerned if children are increasingly detached from the places they inhabit? The biologist E.O.Wilson (1984) *"proposed a genetically based tendency to affiliate with nature, 'biophilia' "* and making the link with well-being. 'Ecopsychology' *"represents a therapeutic orientation which holds that humans need to rediscover their ties to the natural world in order to experience full mental health"*. Per Gustafson quotes Agnew: *"meaningful places emerge in a social context and through social relations, they are geographically located and at the same time related to their social, economic cultural etc surroundings, and they give individuals a sense of place, a 'subjective territorial identity'* (JEP 2001 21 p.6). There is a wealth of material about identification with nature *"there are clearly many people for whom an important aspect of their identity lies in ties to the natural world... or particular geographic locations"* (Clayton and Opotow p.45). A sense of identity and connection allows the individual to then map the local in respect of the global and eventually to have a sense of what Doreen Massey refers to as *"a place of the imagination of longer, deeper temporalities....Place as a passing moment within the depths of time"* (Drew and Kent 2005 p.26). On the larger scale, the concept of environmental identity relates to the sense of how *"our immediate local actions can have global consequences, and that remote environmental threats are personally significant"* (Massey in Drew and Kent 2005 p.61). This may be one of the most compelling reasons for developing an understanding of and connection to nature. However, as Peter Kahn found in interviewing children in a poor area of Houston, *"the majority (84%) said that animals played an important part in their lives, as did plants (87%) and parks or open spaces (70%)* and had a highly developed sense of care about threats to the environment from pollution (Clayton and Opotow 2003 pp.115-116).[18] Robert Sommer has studied the special nature of woods and forests: *"trees not only make economic and physical contributions to human well-being and sense of self, they also contribute in aesthetic, social and psychological ways"* (Sommer in Clayton and Opotow p.180). On a deeper level, many cultures attach spiritual significance to the natural world. Writing about the Koynkon of North Alaska Nelson (1989) states *" According to Koynkon teachers, the tree I lean against feels me, hears what I say about it, and engages me in a moral reciprocity based on responsible use. In their tradition, the forest is both a provider and a community of spiritually empowered beings"* (Kahn in Clayton and Opotow p.123). Jung identified that trees had a special significance for people and collected paintings of trees done by his patients, believing that they were part of the collective unconscious (Sommer in Clayton and Opotow p.194). Environmental awareness in Western culture is sometimes called Ecological identity:

18 The issue for these children was rather one of access to nature, living as they did in an area experiencing high rates of violence and poverty.

"Ecological identities, at least in part, seem to emerge from direct experience in nature that reframe individuals' experiences of themselves in light of a connection to a natural world that is exogenous to culture or society" (Zavetoski in Clayton and Opotow p.300). As in the case of Rachel Carson, this forging of environmental identity often leads to activism *"the knowledgeable citizen whose understanding of the connection between environmental damage and human health leads to forceful action for government regulation of industrial pollution and corporate power"* (Holmes in Clayton & Opotow p.32).

The restorative power of natural and green surroundings has also been studied. Taylor and Kuo examine the evidence for this in relation to children and identified *" compelling evidence for a link between green space and enhanced capacity to pay attention in children"* (Spencer and Blades 2008 p.129). Although rated by their parents, there are links between symptom severity in Attention Deficit Hyperactivity Disorder (ADHD) children and green play spaces with the latter having a positive benefit in contrast with indoor and built outdoor spaces (Spencer and Blades 2008 p.130). This is a finding reinforced by Bagot (2007) who acknowledged *"the restorative capacity of natural environments for children, particularly those with ADHD"* (Malone 2008, pp.10, 21). Using an Attention Deficit Disorder Evalution Scale (ADDES) researchers in Sweden in two nurseries observed children for one year: *"the outdoor nursery children were more attentive, had better powers of memory, were less easily distracted and concentrated on activites for longer"* (Williams-Siegfredsen in Austin 2007 p.69).

Siegel and White (1975) argued that *"locomotor movement within a large scale environment leads to a more accurate and flexible spatial relationship than that produced by physically passive experiences"* and a study by Hart (1981) demonstrated that, *"in general children who walk to school draw more detailed and correctly oriented maps than those who are driven by car or bus"* translating experience directly into observational skills and cognitive ability (Spencer and Blades 2008 p.78). The importance of physical activity for well being both in terms of mental health and avoidance of future health problems like obesity is now accepted. Bente Karlund Petersen, professor of medicine at the Rigshospitalet in Copenhagen University has researched the muscle hormone Interleukin 6 *"which keeps our bodies strong healthy and slim but also has an effect upon our brains, increasing learning and memory"*. He also compared the hamstring muscles of children in indoor and outdoor nurseries and found the latter *"have longer hamstring muscles and that there is a close correlation between muscle development, the brain and social behaviour (Pedersen 2005)"* (Austin 2007 p.70). The advantages of outdoor over indoor learning are also championed by Swedish physician Britt-Louise

32

Theglander citing the importance of movement, memory and the element of risk and pain in stimulating learning, recommending *"that children who are in a learning situation should have movement every ten minutes to achieve optimum brain function in both learning and memory"* (Austin p.71). These are compelling arguments for more outdoor activity and underpinned the Manifesto for Outdoor Learning, but Bailey and Pickup acknowledge that the outdoor context is sometimes *"challenging to the teachers"* whose training and inclination may not suit them to working in this way (Austin p.90).

ART EDUCATION OUTSIDE THE CLASSROOM

Current practice in the UK has benefited from the research work of Sekules, Tickle and Xanthoudaki, Emily Pringle and Engage. Research programmes like en-quire and research undertaken by ACE, CP, now Creativity, Culture and Education (CCE), Guggenheim and Tate have allowed many of the education theories mentioned above to be considered in an arts context. Other contributors from the museum world include Hein, Hooper-Greenhill and Dust. Ken Robinson has also been highly influential through his writing and lecturing, publishing "All our Futures" in 1999 and "Out of Our Minds" in 2001 and promoting a radical rethinking of education practice in schools in favour of creativity.

Hein drew freely on the work of Dewey, Freire, Piaget, Vygotsky and Gardner's Theory of Multiple Intelligences in proposing his own model of the Constructivist Museum. In his continuum of theories of knowledge, Dewey is positioned on the right hand side with an emphasis *"more on practical experience and the application of ideas to action, than to a verbal description of 'truth'"* (Hein, 1998 p.18). The active role of the learner is acknowledged in line with the philosophies of Dewey Piaget and Vygotsky.[19]

Hein identifies the ways in which this approach differs from *"traditional didactic expository education"* (1998, p.25) and clearly articulates both the origins and rationale behind the constructivist approach in contrast with the linear and rigid models of the traditional behaviorist museum. The latter tends to reinforce the dominant culture (white, male, capitalist). Hein argues that "discovery learning" is natural in a museum where value is placed on objects and on learning from objects but warns against simplistic interpretation of this philosophy: *"Monotonous repetitive physical activity, or "mindless" actions are not particularly conducive to mental changes associated with this form of learning, and recent literature has stressed the need for "minds on" as well as "hands on" engagement by learners"* (1998, p.31). Hooper-Greenhill identified that to gain the *"maximum value"* from a museum or gallery visit, reflecting on the experience was critical *"otherwise much of the value will be lost"* (1991, p.120). This highlights the importance of building relationships between gallery or museum and the school, in order to communicate understanding and facilitate the best possible outcomes. However lack of time, the demands of the curriculum and lack of confidence in art teaching have all been identified as reasons why follow up work may not happen (Xanthoudaki in Xanthoudaki et al pp.113- 114). Hein also warns that there are risks involved in an open learning approach, which may help to explain the reasons why change has been slow in the mainstream since there is far more pressure on teachers to deliver set outputs within set time frames: *"the further we move to the right on the learning theory continuum, the less likely it will be that we can expect learners to reach predetermined outcomes"* (1998, p.32).[20] However experimentation and risk taking is crucial to constructivist learning and conclusions must be reached that make sense within the individual's own constructed reality. This will vary according to the individual and takes time.

Hein also discusses research in the museum and identifies the quantitative/qualitative paradigms that have their own associated values and political connotations. He identifies them as stemming from two separate traditions, one statistical the other subjective.

TABLE: ATTRIBUTES OF "EXPERIMENTAL DESIGN" AND "NATURALISTIC" PARADIGMS	
Experimental design	**Naturalistic**
quantitative	qualitative
atomistic	holistic
objective	subjective
laboratory model	real-world based
experimental	naturalistic
hard	soft
confirmatory	exploratory
explanation	understanding
decontextualised	contextual
deterministic	responsive
analytic	synthetic

Fig 2: Reprinted from Hein, George. E., *Learning In The Museum*, 1988 with kind permission of Routledge publishers. Figure 2.4 page 25

He also demonstrates how the early pioneers, like Piaget, who were criticised initially for a personal approach are now fully accepted by proponents of a naturalistic approach that *"acknowledge(s) the inevitable presence of the self and capitalize on the researcher's own perspectives and biases"* (1998, p.69). He ably demonstrates the differences between research approaches and questions the scientific approach as potentially self-limiting and therefore lacking complexity and depth. As Hooper-Greenhill identifies there is a vital connection between the practice and the research methods chosen which: *'say something about our views on what counts as valuable knowledge and our perspectives on the nature of reality'* (Pringle, 2006 p.42).

Hein pleads for networks and not hierarchies among topics and approaches to learning. Together with Hooper-Greenhill, he advocates a naturalistic approach and the importance of practitioner knowledge as critical for professional practice such as teaching. This is a vision for a multi-cultural context and one that accepts other world views and socio-cultural contexts. It is also a realisation that there are many ways in which people do and have preferences for learning and that cultural and learning organisations need to take this into consideration when designing exhibitions or projects. Into this equation comes the interface between the different cultures of school and cultural organisation, teacher and artist, which Sekules eloquently summarises as a need for *"the understanding by one system of the other. It is not a question of assimilation but of collaborative development"* (Xanthoudaki et al, 2003 p.139). This will be examined further in the following chapter.

Contemporary museum and art education practice is precisely concerned with *"the relationship between experience and learning"* and to interrogate aesthetic encounters to *"search for understanding about their meaning, their value, and the processes involved in bringing them about"* (Xanthoudaki et al. p.4). This has been variously translated into approaches which have been well summarised and documented by Emily Pringle in 'Context Process Outcomes' 2006 and discussed in the short term paper 'Ecologies of Practice: Outdoor Learning and the Arts' (Medhurst 2008). CGE can be seen to complement many of the theories and approaches of experiential learning and emerges from a constructivist model of learning that is seen as a highly contextual process (Adams Falk and Dierking in Xanthoudaki et al p.17). Distinct to this approach and in common with experiential learning theory, the concept of Personal Meaning Mapping (PMM) developed by the Institute for Learning Innovation for use in galleries and museums is defined *"PMM is still interested in what a person learns but the focus is on that person's unique 'what' not some prescribed outcome"* (Adams Falk and Dierking in Xanthoudaki et al p.22). Pringle identifies that this is not purely aesthetic or emotional appreciation, but depends upon developing a language, as referenced by Barthes *"looking at art is essentially a cognitive activity that is analogous to deciphering a text"* (Pringle 2006 p.9). Having considered many other existing models from the field, her research led Pringle to propose a learning framework for CGE.[21] The meaning identified in a work of art is seen *"not as an unchanging entity put there by the artist, but as emerging through the active interchange between the artwork and viewer"* (Pringle 2006 p.9). This is very much in tune with the early pioneers and with Hein's clearly defined differentiation between theoretical paradigms that place contemporary practice firmly within the experiential learning tradition. Pringle has described CGE *"as an ongoing and complex process involving individual and collaborative engagement, meaning-making and reflection"* (Pringle 2006, p.41). This is a much more sophisticated form of art education than exists in most schools and highlights the need for continuous professional development and collaborative working which can share skills and practice. Summarised by Hickman as a tension between *"education in art and education through art"* with *"tensions... observed between child and subject centred approaches"* and continuing debates about the relative importance of its aims and values, we can see how Read's theories remain unresolved (Hickman, 2005: 18, Fleming 2010 p.52).

The real life cultural context of CGE offers an opportunity therefore for direct contact both with living artists, contemporary work and experience of the creative process itself, of developing a language for engaging with art in a highly personal way. It involves experimentation and risk taking and because of the nature of contemporary practice, it is often cross-curricular. It addresses critical thinking and enquiry and conforms to what Ken Robinson calls for in *"an education that values different modes of intelligence and sees relationships between disciplines... taught in ways that reflect their intimate connections in the world beyond education"* (2001 p.201). In her recent research article for Tate Papers, Anna Cutler argues that distinctions between informal and formal learning are artificial and that *"it is simply the settings and approaches that differ"* (Cutler 2010 p.2). She calls for more innovation in all contexts, while acknowledging the freedoms enjoyed by the cultural sector in delivering cultural learning: *" that takes place beyond the classroom or lecture theatre, within a cultural setting, and...takes cultural product as its subject matter for direct engagement"* - elsewhere described as "authenticity" (2010 p.4 and Maaria Linko in Xanthoudaki et al p.66). In common with Matarrasso, Cutler identifies many of the benefits and positive outcomes found by cultural learning research in the last ten years such as increased confidence, positive shifts in attitudes and behaviours, improved motivation, and sustained engagement. In common

21 See Appendix 4

with some of the RROL research (Rickinson et al, 2004 p.34) there is also evidence of an increase in critical thinking skills, which can be applied beyond the learning environment.

Distinctively, Cutler defines that *"its content and its approach differ from the established model of education, as cultural and creative learning seeks to generate sustainable skills that can be applied across subjects and education/personal boundaries"* and this is a meta-cognitive approach to learning. Among other observations, she also cites how non-declarative memory plays an important role in creative learning and merits further research and that this form of learning also engages necessarily with emotions in a way that traditional education tends not to (2010 p.7). Cutler highlights the importance of time in terms of meaningful engagement including the notion that there can be delays between an experience and genuine understanding, something identified by Adams Falk and Dierking (Xanthoudaki et al p.17). The next chapter will examine the research findings from FS, CP and other long-term studies, to examine their relevance to the topic and further distil the theory through the lens of practice.

CHAPTER THREE

DISTILLATION

When Charles Darwin was a young man, his father complained about his lack of application to academic studies.:
"I believe that I was considered by all my masters and by my Father as a very ordinary boy, rather below the common standard in intellect. To my deep mortification my father once said to me: 'You care for nothing but shooting, dogs and rat-catching, and you will be a disgrace to yourself and all your family' " (Barlow 1958, p.28).
As history now knows, it was precisely Darwin's love of nature and his observational skills that stimulated his scientific curiosity and changed the course of human knowledge. Evidently his father and the education system of the time did not place value on experiential learning outside the classroom.

In the previous chapter, the relevant theories have been examined. In this chapter these theories will be distilled through looking at available case studies in the arts, cultural and outdoor sectors, before moving to consider the SVA case study. The examples chosen relate to different aspects of this dissertation's topic and they are:

● Creative Partnerships (CP)
● Forest Schools (FS)
● Special Needs Studies
● Galleries

All these contexts have provided the material for long-term research study in an experiential learning context. Art and outdoor learning are referenced in Dr Karen Malone's paper 'Every Experience Matters' written for DCSF and the Farming and Countryside Commission in 2008.[22] The paper was commissioned to support the aims of Every Child Matters and

22 Malone's paper built on the RROL (2004)

'Down Time' Beetle identification

the LOTC manifesto, demonstrating that:

"children engaged in LOTC achieve higher scores in class tests, have greater levels of physical fitness and motor skill development, increased confidence and self-esteem, show leadership qualities, are socially competent and more environmentally responsible"

(Malone 2008, p.4). Malone considered research post 2003 from all over the world including museums and art galleries (2008 p.4). The research was considered in terms of learning, social interactions, emotional well-being, physical experiences and responses, and behaviour change (2008 p.6).[23]

CREATIVE PARTNERSHIPS

CP was launched in 2002 in response to Ken Robinson's All Our Futures report and with a remit to introduce creative learning in schools. The organisation (now CCE) has enjoyed a high level of investment supported by sustained research and evaluation. It is of interest as a context that introduces artists (and others) into the schools. Artists work within the school but also take students outside the classroom.[24] Shirley Brice Heath and Shelby Wolf documented the learning outcomes arising from a project in Hythe Community (Primary) School in Kent in 2004. This involved artist Roy Smith working for one day a week in the school for a year. Entitled *'Visual Learning in the Community School'* the research is also a strong example of a community of learning built through mutual relationships between teachers, school staff, artist, pupils and their families.

The artist used drawing extensively as a means to develop oral language, visual literacy and strategic thinking: "we believe that children's involvement in the arts is cognitive work—a clear activation of the mind as children learn to look at art, engage with materials, and craft as well as reflect on their own creations" (Wolf & Brice-Heath 2004a p.5). The authors show how the children develop their capacity to use metaphor, a particularly rich possibility of all art forms and they show how "the more children develop the ability to focus on the details they see, the greater their capacity for metaphorical language" allowing movement between visual and verbal mental processes (2004a p.9). The children are responding to examples of art taken from books rather than direct experience, however the artist is encouraging them to identify the narratives within the imagery and to express their own feelings in response to them as a means to think about art (2004a p.21). The authors conclude that with these Year 2 children "art builds their cognitive stamina, builds their verbal explanations and offers multiple opportunities for individual as well as thoughtful expression" (2004a p.44).

23 See also Appendix 6: Definitions of Outcomes

24 SVA facilitates outdoor cultural visits for CP on a regular basis and many practitioners work for both organisations

The researchers document the conversations and interactions between the children and the artist, including an exchange where the artist encourages a child to take risks and experiment: "a lot of what you do in art should be accidents, shouldn't it? That's how you learn things"(Wolf & Brice-Heath, 2004b p.6). This directly challenges academic notions of precision in learning curricula and points to the reason that direct experience of the artistic process is important also for teachers. Referencing the work of Roger Shepard in 1988 into the qualities of world-class leaders, they show how as children these individuals become "engrossed in a direct, interactive exploration of...objects and events and [second they did] so unconstrained by conventional verbalized and rigidly compartmentalized interpretations (or dismissals) of these objects or events" (2004b p.6). The authors infer that this points to the need for time allowed for free exploration and to develop verbal and social skills. However it is also critical to develop deliberation as well as accident in the creative process: " the best works of the imagination require intention as well as invention"(2004b p.8). This extends to scientific discovery, as "in the realm of science, accident, even within the confines of well-planned experimentation, opens doors to what could not have been imagined" (2004b pp.10-11). As in the case of Darwin, to return to his example, both scientists and artists can be defined as possessing "curiosity, fascination and mobility of thought" as vital qualities (2004 b p.13).

The authors refer to Csikszentmihalyi and the concept of "flow" or "being fully aware of the content of experience" (2004b p.16). As a corollary to these ideas, however, Roy Smith acknowledges that working in an open process-based way can be alarming to some: "I've noticed that if I do something that is a bit too abstract and chaotic, off the wall, or without rules, then she doesn't necessarily become upset, but she's not very comfortable with it" (2004b p.42). This is an indication that the same approach does not necessarily suit all children, or that they may need more support in feeling comfortable about working in this way. In the Reception class the teachers experimented with child-initiated play and found that the children's behaviour was no longer an issue and in addition to this the SATS results went up (2004c p.13).[25]

By contrast, in his 2008 report on the pedagogy of Creative Practitioners, Maurice Galton from the University of Cambridge faculty of education reflects on the tension often encountered by artists when working with teachers in secondary schools. Citing *"the continued emphasis on target setting and testing"* Galton identifies a *"clash of cultures"* in these encounters, which, he suggests *"may also offer an explanation of why creative practitioners sometimes succeed where schools often appear to fail"* (Galton, 2008 p.10). This occurs precisely where the pedagogical

25 The teachers used research from Reggio Emilia in Italy in this project including diaries

approaches do not match:

"when creative practitioners initially set up situations designed primarily to engineer 'cognitive conflict' so that the pupils are forced to think 'out of the box' teachers are often concerned about the lack of structure which they fear will result in an unacceptable performance" (Galton, 2008 p.33).

This provides an intriguing counterpoint to the situation at Hythe where creativity was actually thought to have had a positive influence on test scores.

Emily Pringle identifies the origin of the artistic pedagogy in participatory and community practice (Pringle, 2008 p.43). Central to the to the artists' expert qualities are *"playfulness, risk taking and productive failure"* together with an understanding that *"art making is necessarily uncertain and fluid"* (ibid p.44). In contrast the teacher has a different role, which involves transmitting information and is focused on precise outputs and performance models of pedagogy. Teacher training, with the possible exception of Foundation Stage, has not always historically encouraged the same approaches to notions of co-learning held by artists *"who question and reorganise their knowledge"* rather than considering themselves *"as infallible experts transmitting information"* (Pringle 2008, p.46). In addition, in the later stages of primary school and at secondary level, the opportunities given to teachers to work in this way are arguably more limited.[26] Pringle defines the difference *"art practitioners can adopt creative and experimental pedagogic models because generally they are free from curriculum constraints whereas teachers are not always at liberty to do so"* the danger here being that the teacher is cast in the role of didact or policeman and the artist as one-off "other" whose intervention is limited (in Galton, 2008 p.47).[27] Pringle suggests that teachers need much more support and professional development to be able to work in co-constructive open ended and collaborative ways.

The emotional aspect of learning for the student was also more highly valued by artists than it was for teachers, who tended to find explanations for pupil disengagement either in terms of pupil deficiency or home, family and peer group rather than in school (Galton, 2008 p.45). However, teachers with more than ten years' experience, significantly, *"tended to explain this deterioration in behaviour on the highly structured nature of today's curriculum"* (Galton, p.54). This paper and the work of Emily Pringle highlight the importance of collaboration and meaningful communication between different pedagogic philosophies. Galton proposes models of increasing expertise to facilitate this, including using Japanese lesson study.[28] He acknowledges that *"Few headteachers saw the creative partnership initiative as a vehicle for changing the school's approach to teaching and learning"* but rather as a

26 See Galton 2008 pp.3 & 4 on pupil satisfaction testing and motivation

27 SG interview

28 See Special needs Studies p.40

means to help cope with 'difficult' pupils or to meet the demands of SEAL and bringing creativity back into the curriculum (2008 p.75). Among Galton's findings is the suggestion that it is only by learning through art practice that teachers *"can remain alive to the possibilities and processes"* and the risk taking involved in a creative learning approach but, equally essentially *" the crucial ideas of joint planning and then reflection on each other's practice"* in other words of meaningful collaboration, were felt to be essential (2008 p.76).

In 'Creative Teaching for Tomorrow', Cremin, Barnes and Scoffham attempt to identify the necessary components for creative teaching using a small study base (2009 p.10).[29] Through identifying a small number of creative teachers, propositions are made that come close to the approach taken by creative practitioners. A model is predicated that suggests collaboration between schools ITE institutions and Creative Partnerships. In interviewing CP practitioners for this dissertation, the school context and the teacher were factors that artists felt could undermine the longer three-year Change programmes:
"The best projects involve the teachers working on an equal footing with the practitioner and the pupils. It is much more interesting if the projects take their own direction and this needs teachers to be willing to change plans as situations change. When the teachers sit back and let the practitioners get on with it the results are never so interesting"
(WG interview).

Practitioners felt that there was more creative freedom working outside and in a context like SVA but that some activities might be better achieved in school.[30] CP's literature suggests that change from within can be complicated without removing the external pressures that determine how teachers may practice. Nonetheless CP programmes demonstrate better academic performance at Key Stages 3 and 4 for the young people involved, although intriguingly no difference at Key Stage 2 (CCE, 2009, pp.15-16).

29. See Appendix 5

30. Interviews WG, CR.

FOREST SCHOOLS

The FS model has been adapted from Scandinavia[31] and involves *"An inspirational process that offers children, young people and adults regular opportunities to achieve, and develop confidence and self-esteem through hands-on learning experiences in a woodland environment"* (O'Brien & Murray 2006 p.6). This includes:

- Regular contact over a long period of time and in all weathers, involving a weekly or fortnightly session at an optimum 15 minutes travel time from the site
- A high ratio of adults to children or young people and small groups
- Links to the National Curriculum involving creative approaches aimed at stimulating curiosity and motivation to learn
- Whole child multi-sensory approach
- Teachers involved closely writing the learning resources

O'Brien and Murray's 2006 report, commissioned by the FC and Forest Research, looked at two phases involving one group of children in Wales linking the FS methodology to its impact on individual children and a second phase tracking a small number of children in England over an eight-month period. The approach is firmly based in action research, aiming at a *"full integration of action and reflection and on an increased collaboration between all those involved in the inquiry project"* (2006 p.10). Since FS works with small group numbers they are sometimes selective about participants. The phase 1 cohort involved an early years 'nurture' group with special needs and a Year 6 cohort including kinaesthetic children, those who might be vulnerable in transition, perhaps lacking support at home and consciously not including those with special needs (in this instance) or any participants liable to display strong behaviour that might 'squash' others (2006 p.11). FS identifies that their approach has particular value and importance *"where individuals have not been able to benefit and thrive in other educational settings"* (2006 pp.6-7). Termed appreciative inquiry after Elliott (1999) the aim is to encourage and bring about behavioural change challenging *"the traditional problem-solving approach to change that views systems as faulty machines with parts needing to be fixed. Instead it encourages the view that an exploration and affirmation of what works in a system is a more effective and sustainable way to maximise effective performance"*(2006 p.11).

The evaluation outcomes for Phase 1 illustrate many of the theoretical research findings about the effects of contact with Nature:

31 It began in the 1950s and came to Britain in the 1990s (O'Brien & Murray p.7).

- having positive social outcomes (self esteem and self confidence)
- co-operative working and increased awareness of others

46

● counters lack of motivation and negative attitudes to learning
● encourages ownership and pride in the natural environment
● better relationship with and understanding of the outdoors
● increases skills and knowledge of participants (2006 p.13).

Phase 2 included additional cognitive criteria and more detail in terms of:

● social skills
● development of language and communication skills, mark-making
● physical and motor skills
● motivation and concentration
● knowledge and understanding (2006 p.14).

Evaluation materials involved triangulation and included observations made by teachers and parents or carers (2006 p.15). Findings indicated particular benefits in terms of children with EBD (2006 p.33) and ADHD (2006 p.20). FS's holistic approach extends to involving parents and carers in the co-learning and identifies the ways in which it meets the agenda of Every Child Matters (2006 pp. 42 & 45). The importance for the teacher of seeing children in another context, away from the classroom, is also highlighted as being of importance and as having an influence back in the classroom (2006 p.41).[32] This report called for mainstreaming of FS in early years and extending the model, which also involves the training of teachers as forest school practitioners, in order to extend the benefits for children's health and well-being. Examining the FS study, Malone identifies *"The value of this type of approach is its replicability and comparability"* (2008, p.24). Current changes and the challenges of funding such intensive programmes may threaten their widespread adoption, in spite of the evidence. FS identifies some of the issues here:

"Some schools are struggling with funding and cannot afford to transport children to Forest School; they are bringing the philosophy into their school grounds by creating more natural areas. While this is a good idea, woodlands have a particular advantage over other habitats as their structure and layout allows for greater adventure and mystery. For example, woodland provides greenery and cover affording opportunities to hide and create secret places, a feature that can be particularly important for a child's development"
(Guldager and Agervig Carstensen, 2004; Thomas and Thompson, 2004; O'Brien, 2004; O'Brien, 2005) (2006 p.45).

32 A finding reflected in the primary research and interviews with artists and teachers

33 Interview AW

In the case of a FS practitioner who works at Canterbury Environmental Education Centre (CEC) this has been tackled by purchasing a minibus. The scheme is currently subsidised by the LEA and therefore the charge is £30 per hour plus a fee for the use of the minibus.[33] Many FS schemes are supported by grants, for example the one at Shorne Country Park through the DFES now the DE. The groups are very small (no more than 15 in the case of CEEC) and the emphasis is on long term regular contact to allow familiarity and trust to develop, with the woodland site and the adults the children are working with. Inset sessions are recommended to teachers taking part in FS.

It is worth noting that in Scandinavia the integration of outdoor learning in schools is common and has been supported for many years.[34]

SPECIAL NEEDS STUDIES

Other studies point to the particular value of environment based learning for special needs children. Using the Japanese practice of lesson study,[35] teachers and researchers conducted a two-year investigation for NFER at the Chelsea Group of Children (CGC) published in 2009. Using David Lazear's work on 'naturalist intelligence' as a framework and in common with the best experiential learning practice, they incorporated reflection as a vital part of the learning process. Reflection was supported through the use of filming, training, peer-review, discussion and conversations to embed the findings in the nature-based curriculum (Duemler, Hartman & Sanders 2009, p.57). The team used pupil progress data, observations (film and photographic) and pupils' work as evidence. The children had a preference for visual learning and some were non-verbal. The team aimed to have an impact on the children's engagement in respect of their skills in:

- vocabulary and expression
- visual attention
- comprehension
- motivation to complete problem solving tasks
- engagement with learning

The findings were positive *"we have recognized the benefits that connecting with the natural world can bring to our community of special needs children"* and the impacts were felt both in terms of *"our children academic profiles and our own professional development"* (Duemler Hartman & Sanders, 2009 p.58). The findings also showed how *"the environmental context is not only a good integrator of subject areas, but also...of best practices in education"* (Monroe and Ernst, 2006 12: 3 p.430). This small study has also produced further materials including a dokuwiki to be shared with colleagues and practitioners wishing to use a nature based curriculum (Duemler, Hartman & Sanders 2009, p.62). It is an excellent example of collaborative enquiry and creative teaching

34 Summary in Fjortoft and Sageie (2000) in Landscape and Urban Planning 48, p.84

35 Also mentioned in the CP paper as a means for catering for individual learning needs (Galton 2008 p.76)

taking place without the need for huge resources but by integrating a research approach in the whole school ethos. *"This experiential process has drawn previously silent children towards speech, offers a framework for reflection and rewarding opportunities to apply their knowledge"* (Duemler Hartman & Sanders, 2009 p.58).

GALLERIES

Malone found that work on school grounds and museums provided the best results for her study, with the research on galleries tending to be *"one-off and small in number"* although she acknowledged a growing body of research evidence (2008 p.9). Malone's findings concerning the arts only found outcomes in the social domain with *"no results found to support emotional benefits"* (2008, p.13). On closer scrutiny this is based on a study into out of school activities with music, drama and opera. The Champions of Change report by Edward Fiske finds that the programmes appeal to hard to reach groups and:

"provide powerful evidence that on the highest levels of literacy, in the realms of social and personal growth and development, and in the development of high-order thinking skills, the arts provide an ideal setting for multi-faceted and profound learning experiences (Fiske 1999: 86)" (Malone 2008 p.19).

Museum and art museum studies used control groups and found outcomes in terms of critical thinking skills and better academic performance in the 'Thinking Through Art" project (pp.14-15). In the museum project cited, students motivation, emotional and social well-being and improved assignment marks for a museum-related project were outcomes (Box 2, p.15). Malone mentions that several studies show that cognitive impacts often have associated benefits in terms of behaviour, affective learning and long-term memory (2008, p.15). It is arguable that the groups Fiske is discussing may have benefited emotionally for example in terms of enhanced self-concept or increased self-esteem, merely that the social benefits were the focus.

The researcher Les Tickle articulates the importance of understanding evidence-based practice: *"theory relationship, the place of social action in relation to knowledge, and the extent to which action is linked with or itself constitutes research"* (Xanthoudaki et al 2003, p.168). He advocates a model where "organic intellectuals" somewhat akin to creative practitioners, can develop research processes with students using the gallery as the site for research with the role of the teacher defined as the "professional intellectual" (Xanthoudaki et al, 2003 p.181).

En-quire, a research programme run by Engage the association for Gallery education, has now been running since 2004. The programme was based on the idea of 'clusters' involving partnerships of schools or youth groups, galleries, artists, teachers and a higher education partner *"to bring structure and rigour to the research"* (Taylor ed. 2008 p.7). Phase 2 (2006 – 2008) involved seven clusters and listed in the key findings:

- participants found the projects more stimulating and involving than other learning experiences and therefore were better motivated putting in more effort and commitment
- developed self confidence and had a sense of achievement
- encouraged new visiting for galleries and opportunities for a richer cultural life
- introduction to contemporary art practice and values, confidence in talking about and experimenting with the process of making art
- learned art skills particularly in digital media increasing career options
- life skills independent working, decision making, social skills, communication debate and discussion of ideas, team working, risk taking and experimentation
- working with artists to encourage questioning, experimentation and process over product, different possibilities and ways of thinking as distinct from work with teachers
- artists worked as facilitators and co-learners, mutual trust developed
- CPD for artists and teachers offered opportunities for mutual reflection

The research involved 182 projects, 124 schools, 39 galleries, 172 artists and benefited more than 7360 young people and has since involved three further clusters including Kent (SVA, Turner Contemporary and Canterbury Museums Service from 2007). In common with the other partners, the project has strengthened the cultural infrastructure both locally as well as nationally and allows the research to be shared through international networks.

The focus is on engagement with young people and *"several of the projects have involved young people at risk of inclusion, with difficult or disadvantaged backgrounds, or with behavioural difficulties"* (Taylor ed. 2008, p.10). This reinforces Fiske's finding that art both *"reaches children who are not being reached"* and provides opportunities for *"developing a learning community between adults and children"* (Malone, 2008 p.19). These groups are the focus of current en-quire research, which complements SVA's 'Down Time' project that has provided the primary

50

research material for this dissertation. In addition the en-quire research has looked in depth at:

- the roles of artists and teachers in terms of how each profession can add value to the other
- how long term relationships can be established between galleries artists and schools
- how self directed learning can be stimulated encouraged and sustained

In terms of longitudinal study, the remit and project targets set by DCMS and DFES (now DE) have shifted with every funding round but nonetheless has allowed the research to continue for six years ending in March 2011. The communities of learning and the overarching opportunities for sharing best practice that have been created are vital in terms of developing potential and understanding of the complex interactions between epistemology and ontology. The weakness, in terms of Malone and similar researcher's criteria are the lack of control groups and of clear educational outcomes that can easily be translated into mainstream criteria and mapped onto a framework like her own[36] or that used by FS. However many of the groups are not in mainstream and in terms of learning engagement, the outcomes have been positive with many participants studying for flexible qualifications like Arts Award.[37]

COMMONALITIES AND DIFFERENCES

Between the aforementioned examples there are commonalities and differences.
The commonalities are that they:

- Are experiential and reflective
- Include elements of risk (exploratory/ open-ended/ outside classroom)
- Constructivist/ co-constructivist
- Long-term
- Funding dependent
- Pay attention to the role of well-being in learning
- Have a high adult:pupil ratio
- Environmental (& art) settings selective or aimed at areas of need (ADHD, kinaesthetic learners, autistic, vulnerable)
- Similar approach as that used in progressive and "alternative" educational settings or where mainstream approach "isn't working" viz SEAL and Leuven

36 Appendix 7

37 See Bentley 1998 p.83 on off-site learning and engagement

Learning outcomes include:

- Development of problem-solving and critical thinking skills[38]
- Independent/appreciative enquiry
- Engagement (and improved behaviour)
- Improved skills in language, vocabulary, expressive, motor, health
- Imaginative work
- Improved motivation, social skills, tolerance, self esteem, well-being

The differences are:

- Forest schools model has clear replicability & comparability, close teacher involvement, frequent activity, 15 minute travel time to woodland site
- CP programmes delivered largely in schools by artists and other practitioners
- Galleries work with artists: visits both guided and unmediated: formal and informal groups: teacher resources and CPD, growing research base
- Strong evidence in environmental based learning on benefits with mental health and well-being (specifically ADHD)[39]

This demonstrates a growing, strong body of evidence, which is finding that experiential education and learning do have particular benefits and outcomes. The commonalities and learning outcomes show that there may be a link between time and regularity of contact with successful outcomes.[40] Alternative approaches can have unexpected outcomes that include academic benefits. Approaching learning in a holistic and integrated way often leads to positive outcomes for all concerned and a shift in approach can unlock learning. All the examples given above depend on an approach that regards the site of learning as an opportunity for research. It can no longer be claimed that the evidence does not exist but rather, that a new and radical approach is needed to build on this. This should include more support for teachers, artists, outdoor settings and cultural organisations to work together using a consistent and sustained approach allowing for "rigorous doubt" to be better understood and applied (Pringle 2008, p.42).

38 See Monroe and Ernst 2006 (p.438).

39 Taylor and Kuo's work referenced by Malone 2008 (p.10).

40 Medhurst (2008 p.11)

CHAPTER FOUR

SVA CASE STUDY: *DOWN TIME*

The primary research for this dissertation represents one strand of SVA's education and learning programme, funded through chances4change (C4C) and the health authority. C4C is a £5.6m portfolio of 62 projects in the South East funded by the Big Lottery Fund Well-being programme. The project targets 'at risk' groups with the aim of addressing and improving well-being (http://www.wellbeingsoutheast.co.uk/chances4change/). Down Time began its research and development phase in 2008 and Phase 1 of the project took place in April and May 2009. This involved the training of artists, teachers, teaching assistants, care and social workers to work with particular groups. The participants in Phase 1 were:

- Hearing Impairment Unit (HIU) in mainstream primary
- Young Carers
- East Kent Health Needs Education Service (EKHNES)
- Young Offenders (YOT)

Film, reflective journals, and sound recordings were used for the evaluations and this involved everyone on the research project, including the artists, teachers, teaching assistants, care and social workers and participants. SVA commissioned a film-maker to document Phase 1, create a film as an advocacy tool, and to be a member of the research team.[41] The film and audio materials are presented on disc and will be referred to in the text as evidence. Where the young people are quoted these are audio, written and verbal responses. A sample session plan is included in Appendix 8.

41 The film is subtitled with the hearing impaired children in mind as well as one of the artists who is deafened.

A holistic approach to creating a community of enquiry and co-learning was considered fundamental to the project's philosophy. The training

54

was designed specifically with the participant groups and context in mind and involved specialists in each field. Support was received from the University of Southampton and from the national portfolio staff, with sustainability as an ongoing theme of C4C.

Phase 2 was to have involved groups from Phase 1 (excluding the HIU)[42] providing some continuity in the primary research material. Adjustments were made giving a more regular schedule of dates to the YOT group with the aim of teaching transferable skills allied with the sculpture maintenance programme. The maintenance activity had been very popular with YOT in Phase 1. Young Carers and EKHNES were involved but owing to recruitment problems with the YOT service (an unusually high number of young people were on remand and therefore unavailable) alternatives had to be found at short notice. Changes had to be negotiated with the funder and approved by the Lottery. This resulted in only 2 of the 3 groups from Phase 1 carrying on as YOT were unable to fulfill their commitment. It should be added that continuity of the team working with the Young Carers was also disrupted when the support team was made redundant very suddenly and so the working relationships that had been established were lost. Although the manager was prepared to stand in for colleagues, she was also subsequently made redundant and the last date of this strand was lost. To recap, the groups finally involved in Phase 2 were:

- EKHNES
- Young Carers
- Special school[43]
- Year 6 transition primary school group

Three of the six artists involved in Phase 1 were involved in Phase 2 with support and mentoring from an experienced SVA project manager.[44]

The evaluation framework was devised for Phase 2 in response to Dr Malone's paper and adapted to include other materials relevant to the well-being agenda. It was designed to capture as wide a range of possible outcomes allowing material to be filtered on the broad range of research themes found in the secondary research.[45] This document was shared with the artists, teachers, care and social workers. The permission of all the participants was sought in terms of film, photographic and audio permissions and research. In view of the vulnerable nature of many of the young people and the sensitivity of the material, their identities are protected in the text; individuals are referred to by initials and the group they belong to. It should be noted that some of the settings were non-formal and that for example the Young Carers' sessions in Phase 2 were part of respite and took place in the school holidays. Where

42 This decision was made due to capacity and funding

43 This material has not been included mainly due to space constraints

44 A third phase will take place in 2010/11 with YOT

45 See Appendix 1 Field Notes Guide

Down Time team at *Superkingdom*: training May 2009

possible, some additional evaluation exercises were conducted with the participant groups.

The issues encountered highlight some of the problems facing practitioners working with 'at risk' groups and indeed manifest the wider risks involved in these projects. Research ideally requires continuity in order to be able to draw conclusions because of the intricate web of relationships involved and disruptions and changes can compromise outcomes and comparability. It must be remembered however, that every situation involving human beings is fluid and dynamic.

The first phase of the project included two days of training at SVA, involving the artists and the teachers, care and social workers from each group, the first theoretical, the second practical and based in the forest working with the learning manager, an ecologist from AONB and an artist involved with education at SVA for many years. Maggie Anwell, a psychotherapist and consultant leading the training for the artists working with the young carers and EKHNES,[46] articulated the ethos of the project;

"Inclusion is essential to everyone's self respect. Many people in our society feel excluded from art making which ought to be their heritage and their right" (DT film disc 1: 4.46 – 5.02).

The aims were articulated as encouraging reflective practice and sharing, fostering creativity through doing, observing, listening and taking time. SVA director Sandra Drew spoke about the parallel approaches of the commissioning and learning in the organisation (DT film disc 1: 2.04 – 2.32). Invited to choose an object as from the forest, artist Will Gould selected a budding fern to convey his ideas to the group:
"I just love that it's got all this potential about to happen, it's all there ready to unfold. I also love that it's got the idea of the forest being messy and disordered and yet it's such a perfect little package in there; it holds both those ideas for me" (DT film disc 1: 2.44-3.05).

Approaching the primary research held much in common with this metaphor and the process of reflecting on the material in the light of the main question was again one of trying to find threads in the labyrinth. The evaluation materials are enormous. The groups are both formal and informal and the age range extends from 5 to 18 years. As the process went on, certain recurring themes began to emerge and suggested the way in which the question of what is the value of experiential learning in a Land Art context might be answered. What follows is both narrative and selected material. This will be presented in the sequence of YOT, Young Carers, and EKHNES, followed by Cheriton and the Year 6

46 The groups were paired because of issues with low numbers, but this was reviewed in Phase 2 following the experience of Phase 1

primary transition group from Phase 2. The evidence will then be further examined by considering the views of teachers, artists and practitioners interviewed for this dissertation.

YOT: Phase 1 only

Two day long sessions May 2009

4 young people attended but only 2 for both days: one due to ill health another opted out

The young people involved were new into the youth offending system but also one individual who had just come out of prison

The age range was 14 – 18 years

The aim was to engage the young people with art and with the natural environment

One of the artists working with this group was deafened, so deaf awareness was part of both the training and the ground rules for the young people around mutual respect and listening

---

One of the common themes for this group was that of play, which seemed to correlate with comments made by the social worker and both of the artists:
"I think she's getting out of this what she's not had in her childhood. Now she's being allowed to play. I've never seen her like this and she's chatting and she's happy it just proves what can happen when you're out in these spaces" (DT film disc 1: 19.23 and making 19.39).

58

The value of play for individuals who have been forced to grow up too fast was identified in Neil's reflective journal:
"What resonated with me most was how these young people came to the woods looking pale and withdrawn but through the course of the day became more animated and playful. This resulted in lots of smiles and laughing and colour in the cheeks" (NK)

and Pauline reflects on their immaturity and how it manifests:

"I was interested to observe low level capacity for frustration that these young people have, and their real neediness for things to go in the way they want. They seem stuck in a very young developmental stage and their lack of good enough parenting is obvious" (PA).

A different young woman is also seen making a floor-based sculpture, using mud and water to make the materials stick, she is clearly enjoying herself and she says:
"It's a bit dirty, but it's worth it" (DT film disc 1: 22.08 – 22.25).

Enjoyment both of the forest and of the making and maintenance activities and self- esteem were also recurrent themes. Lack of confidence led the young girl to say that she could not draw, but she is seen on film making a beautiful drawing of the Richard Harris sculpture, even as she is saying this (DT film disc 1: 17.19 – 17.58) (researcher's notes) In an email sent after the project had ended, the social worker writes about her:
"I loved her time there and would love to come back it really did loads for her self esteem and she has not really got over the way you were all so kind to her. That's when you no (sic) the work has been a success when they talk about it" (From social worker 4 June 2009 21:20:18)
Two of the young people say to camera that they would like to return (DT film disc 1: 22.46 - 22.55) and Neil notes that one young person said to him: *"I thought it was gonna be shit but it was alright"*(NK).

The effect of the forest was also referenced as already seen in the social worker's observation about the change that can be made possible *"in these spaces"*. Neil commented that *"the chaos of the young people's everyday life was not reflected in the forest"* observing that *"the forest does require different codes of behaviour* (NK).
The individual who left after lunch on the first day clearly did not respond positively to the forest. He has ADHD and had just come out of prison. The art he encountered was outside his experience and not to his liking. He found the living arch sculpture by Richard Harris *"a mess"* (researchers journal). The artists and researcher all reflected that the vast space and unfamiliarity were probably too difficult a contrast with the

60

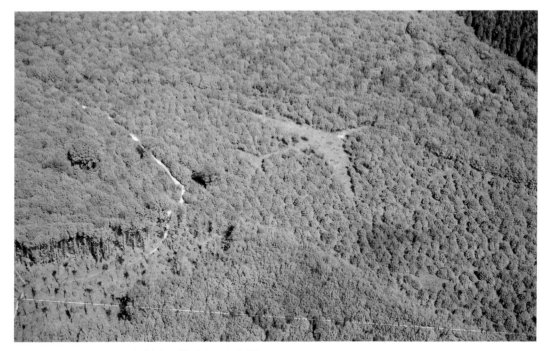

Aerial view of Rosie Leventon's *B52*

order and structure of prison and this was an individual who evidently found it hard to trust and decided the experience was not for him.

The other young man did engage with the experience and displayed sensitivity, enjoyment, creativity and many skills. This individual's engagement can be seen on film. Guessing the shape of the B52 is an aeroplane demonstrating cognitive awareness of space (DT film disc 1: 18.20 – 18.28).

Listening to Jem's piece and smiling, showing enjoyment of the sound sculpture and the concepts behind it (18.57-19.15). Talking about football and about the title for his piece the Wind Reader (20.05 – 20.38) and speaking about the nest sculpture *"I thought of it last night when I was at home"* (20.52 – 21.10).

Both sculptures were sophisticated pieces of work.[47] His approach was thoughtful and he spoke up for Richard Harris' piece when others voiced scepticism *"It's a good idea"* (17.09 – 17.13). This individual also expressed an interested in getting involved in the maintenance programme and was made an offer to continue supporting the sculpture warden after the project ended (researcher journal).

47 See Illustrations p.61

Top: Wind Reader
Below: PA reflective journal

Nest

Having witnessed this potential, it was unfortunate that he was subsequently sent to prison for 4 months and in spite of communication via the social worker ensuring him the offer would be held for him, he completely disengaged after his release. The team made many references to their own learning on the project and felt strongly that the difficulties of working with the group were outweighed by the achievements. This may be best summed up by Neil's comment: *"I felt that this experience was powerful for me and believe that the young people took something away with them that they will remember even if it is not in the immediate future"*(NK).

Young Carers: Phases 1 & 2

Phase 1 two days Phase 2-3 sessions planned, only 2 realised

There were only 3 in the Young Carers Group in Phase 1 mixed with young people from EKHNES but this was reviewed for Phase 2

There were 13 young people in the group for Phase 2 but no continuity
1st Visit: 12 x young people aged 13 – 17 (7 x boys & 5 x girls)
2nd Visit: 8 x young people aged 13 – 17 (4 x boys & 4 x girls)

The longitudinal study was disrupted due to redundancies in the service

The aim was to provide respite for the young people from their caring responsibilities

Because of the informal setting and the limited contact time the support workers have with the young people, evaluation material was limited to the film observations and the reported conversations with artists, researcher and care workers. Some audio content is also included.

Play and the change in body language with this group recur again. One young man in Phase 1 demonstrates this most powerfully. This individual has ADHD but he responded very positively to the forest environment and his engagement can be seen on film. Talking to the team (DT film: Disc 1: 11.20). Listening to Jem Finer's sound sculpture and smiling (11.26 – 11.30), in common with the young man in the YOT group. He chose to build a runway with the help of a friend on Day 1 ending in a pile of leaves, which he raked together and then jumped into (12.20 – 12.38). *"R said on the way home in the minibus that he loved it all but especially liked jumping in leaves!! "* (Support worker email 12 May 2009 10:49:51).

This individual's natural tendency towards performance was borne out on Day 2 when he made himself a crown of bluebells and sat inside the 3D sculpture his group had made (15.52 – 15.56). Further insight came when talking to the Young Carers Support manager on the second visit to the forest in Phase 2, a year later:
"He's a changed boy, however difficult they seem to start with because some of them are difficult, every child has a hook and it's finding that thing. He spent all that time making that pile of leaves he jumped in. He still has his moments but he's so much easier and nicer" (Disc 2: A2 0.38 – 1.04).

Time has also played a part in this transformation:

"We worked with him for a couple of years before that quite intensively and we're still working with him now but you can see it every once in a while something kerching and I looked at him and thought we've got him. It wasn't straight away but that's because of his thought processes and his reflection" (Disc 2: A2 1.47 – 2.17).

Asked why she thought it had worked she said: *" it's having the opportunity, he's the man at home he has a lot of responsibility and a lot going on but it was like giving him permission to run around, be a 12 year old and play in the woods"* (Disc 2: A2 2.53 – 3.13).

This individual was also proud to have his sculptures praised by professional artists who could talk to him about contemporary art performance pieces. The benefit of play and freedom in the outdoors is reiterated and seems to have had a transformative effect that has outlasted the time span of the project.

Enjoyment of the natural environment and enjoyment were reinforced in the feedback about S who: *"also said how much he enjoyed being outdoors and would like to go back to the woods"* (Support worker email 12 May 2009 10:49:51). The young people were proud of their achievements and found inspiration in the works of art they saw: "C *was really inspired by the art work and couldn't wait to show her mum the photos of her work"* (Support worker email 12 May 2009 10:49:51).

This individual also overcame some personal challenges:
"I recall on the second day that one of the young carers was flagging after the long walk the day before. Her mother is agoraphobic and she is in danger of developing the same condition as she never goes out. All the walking and fresh air must have been very demanding. When we were at the Cloud Chamber she said she didn't think she could cope but in the end she was the one who led the practical activity and got involved, even leading the boys" (researchers journal and DT film Disc 1: 15.23 – 15.45).

The beneficial effects of the forest and of being outdoors were strongly evidenced in Phase 2. In Phase 1 it was noted that attention spans improved when the young people were engaged in making. Young people found being in the forest both calming and inspiring. S lives in a place where a lot of construction is going on and said that he found the scenery relaxing (Disc 2: Relaxation 0.9 – 0.15) He goes on to say: *"this place gives me hope that we're not destroying everything"* and he talks about his concern for the environment (Disc 2: Hope 0.5 – 0.7). Fran reported that *"he says he's just so happy when he's in this environment"* and he had identified that six different places in the forest where he would like to build a home. Another individual *"said he feels so happy when he's in the wood, he stops feeling angry"* (Disc 2 LF2: 0.9 – 0.13). One individual imagined stories associated with the B52 about a plane crash landing in the forest. This boy also fantasised about selling his drawings and elaborated on reality, imagining a castle on the site of Dominique Bailey's sculpture. His creative storytelling may also have evolved partly as a way to cope with the hardships of everyday life and develop resilience.

The group of 3 girls acknowledged that although they had been to the forest before, it was the first time they had been able to absorb what it was all about, showing that they had benefited from spending time and having a mediated experience. This group also included two cousins who befriended another girl. Due to the isolation of these young people, forming social networks and friendships is significant for them.

EKHNES Phases 1 & 2

Phase 1 two consecutive days May 2009
Phase 2 three sessions March – June 2010

There were 9 young people involved in Phase1 and two of them also took part in Phase 2 of a total of 14 students from Year 10

Some have come through Young Person Units (residential mental health clinics) and 3 of the group we worked with in Phase 2 were in the same unit for 6 months plus

The aim was to support their art work and in Phase 2 the GCSE coursework around natural forms

---

Perhaps due to the formal setting and the fact that the group were studying art, the engagement with art making and meaning making was stronger for this group. Play was evidenced in Phase 1 when the group made their own performance piece from found materials (DT disc 1:14.48). One of the artists commented that the young people's work exceeded her expectations and *"The performance art works in particular captured for me youth, vitality, magic, and myth along with a sense of belonging. The 2D and 3D artworks were unique, intricate, they showed diversity in shape, colour, and texture"* (reflective journal). The theme of enjoyment comes through in the young people's evaluations. The

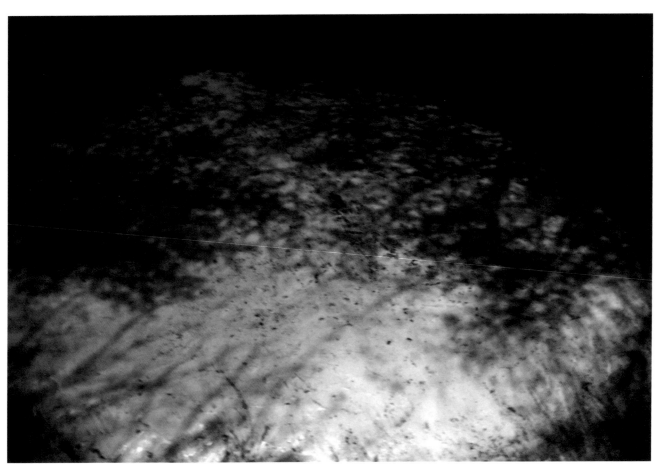

Image from Chris Drury *Coppice Cloud Chamber*, 1998

following statement shows an appreciation for working alongside the artists: *"I think the best part of the day was making our own sculptures, I really enjoyed that because for a couple of days we was put in the shoes of professionals. You have given us a really wonderful experience and we all appreciate it"*.

The students reflected on their own learning and on the use of unfamiliar media and techniques, which seemed to stimulate their creativity: *"It's a lot easier than working with pencils and that because you can use your imagination"*. They also appreciated the physicality of working outside: *"It's like you get more imagination out here because you're doing stuff with your hands"*. They found that there were challenges but enjoyed overcoming them: *'Whilst making our models I helped to cut down wood which was difficult but also fun"*.

Direct experience of the art works and in particular the Coppice Cloud Chamber by Chris Drury, was also inspiring for the young people (and this was a theme that recurred in Phase 2). Comments were:
"My favourite piece of art was the cloud chamber. I thought the way that you could see the shadows moving on the white surface was unexplainable"

"I partically enjoyed going into the caprice (sic) *chamber. I loved the way it was made and how the trees swayed on the cold stone it was like the cinemas"*

These remarks show how the experience of the sculptures has captured the imagination of the young people and evoked a sense of wonder. The same holds for comments about the forest itself, in terms of beauty and scale:
"The forest was very beautiful. I was surprised how big it was....Your job must be wonderfull to see the forest throughout the season.....I was happy I learnt how to weave. It was a very nice experience very active and imaginative."

One student, talking about the work he created on the theme 'safeguarding', explains the thought process behind his making, showing a deeper appreciation of the environment and an understanding of ecology:
"it represents the forest because everything that's in there is from the forest" (DT film disc 1:13.02 – 13.50).
Continuing Phase 2 with EKHNES gave the best opportunity for longitudinal study and was felt to be successful by the teachers and the SVA team. The young people reflected that they had enjoyed the experience and gained from it. The teacher felt it had enhanced the group's GCSE work. The longer time frame allowed relationships to be built on and issues discussed and understood so that deeper co-learning

EKHNES building showing outdoor space (within fenced area)

took place. It should be mentioned that the Year 10 group was considered to be particularly difficult by the school, which had employed new members of staff to deal with some of the attendant behavioural issues.

One of the emergent themes, both from the reflective journal and the interview with the teacher, was that of difference and contrast between the school environment and that of the forest:
"The things I had in mind were coming through with the children when I spoke to them. A feeling of being at one with the world. The forest provided solace and comfort. The school is a really confined space, it's a pen, a rabbit hutch it's so confined for the children with their problems – there's nowhere else for them to go" (JP interview)[48]

48 Links between physical space and behaviour Horne Martin in Spencer and Blades 2006 p.92

One student wrote:
"The atmosphere when walking through the woods was very welcome and I enjoyed being in open space" related to this is the fact that this

student was at the Unit because he had Osgood's Schllater's disease. This condition occurs in teenagers and often those who play a lot of sport and it can be very debilitating:
"I loved the first visit when I made that football shape with all the natural resources".

One month later in the follow up evaluation exercise, he records*: "my favourite thing was when me and R did that football shape on the floor".* J spoke a great deal about having to give up football and not being allowed back to his school due to his illness. He also reflected to his teacher that on coming to the unit *"My head was messed up with medication".* The piece he created had personal significance for him. According to the teacher it had also led to a friendship between the two boys, which was one of the unexpected outcomes of the project (JP reflective journal and interview*).*

Another unexpected outcome occurred when a group of girls worked together really well. Both they and the teacher reflected that much of this would not have happened in school. Again the reflective material points to a sense of freedom and "flow" (Csikzsenthmihalyi) in their making: *"they went with their free thoughts and the flow"* (JP interview).

Another individual spoke to the teacher about how the forest was both calming and inspiring: *"She hears voices. She said "being busy in the forest meant her mind was being kept busy she wasn't dwelling on matters, she was able to relax and forget about things, she felt it was calming easier for the mind to think and focus and at times she felt totally lost in her ideas"* (JP interview) It was significant for the teacher that the students said about being in the forest*: "it freed up our minds"* (JP interview).

Identification with the forest as inspiration was evidenced through other student comments, two on writing in response to Hamish Fulton's work:
"To me being in the forest inspires me to write as if the forest is talking to me"
"I also thoroughly enjoyed the creative writing about the forest. It was easier to come up with ideas to create a picture of the setting" Two students particularly liked this activity and another was prompted to begin writing poetry as a result.

Another reflection identifies more with the sculptural work: *"It really gave us a chance to connect with the forest and focus more on what I am doing".* This indicates the ability to concentrate better away from school.
"I really enjoyed seeing all the art sculptures. The woods have given me some great ideas for my art"
"I enjoyed the fresh air and being able to admire other artists work"
One post project comment made in response to the question, "Something you have learnt*" was "It's easier to be creative"* and another individual

also managed to produce sustained work in charcoal, a medium she is not keen on:
"She is very creative but normally would give up easily. She will tear work out of her sketchbook. She said 'I kept going'."(JP interview) Another individual also identified the importance of novelty and of developing resilience:
"I learnt that I can try new things and improve with practice".

There were comments about the use of natural materials and of tools. Several students overcame personal phobias and developed confidence as a result of coping with them and with challenges presented by the environment. There were positive aspects to their experiences of dealing with insects, a dislike of dirt and so on that were perhaps unusually powerful for this group. Another unexpected outcome resulted from an incident with smoking (forbidden in the forest), which led to one individual giving up smoking (JP interview). One of these students found the forest soothing and she felt calm and not nervous and felt more confident about coping with the fear of having a seizure out of school as a result. She also overcame a fear of heights and was able to negotiate a stile "I never thought I would be able to do what I did" (Student evaluation & JP interview).

Students and teacher appreciated working with artists. JP felt it had supported and enhanced her practice as an art teacher. For the young people, they found it refreshing and encouraging working with artists:
"The artists made the forest work for us" (JP interview and reflective journal). One student was particularly pleased that Tonita shared her art journal and felt privileged to be shown it. The young people liked being treated as equals: "I liked being included and involved in all the activities as I usually wouldn't bother" J commented that he was with very positive people and he appreciated 'that they were encouraging and not reminding me to get on' although he did not enjoy the writing exercise. The teacher emphasised the importance for this group of having conversations with new people because: "many of these young people can easily shut themselves down"(JP interview). Academically and for the purposes of their GCSE coursework, direct contact with art and artists was important. One individual who has ADHD and had worked on the project for both phases brought in his sketchbook on the last session to share with the team and allowed his mind maps to be photographed (researchers notes and JP interview).

These were the source of many ideas and the teacher reflected that this was of huge significance for R because he would normally find personal disclosure very difficult. "Art has been an area that has really allowed him to come out of himself. He is really proud of his art work" (JP interview).

73

EKHNES group working on *Hill Seat*, Tim Norris, 1995

R mind maps

Working with people who did not have preconceptions about the young people was also felt to be of value by the teacher.

The risks of working with vulnerable young people in an outdoor environment were more evident in Phase 2, perhaps because of the more extended time line. In spite of this both SVA team, teaching staff and students had overwhelmingly positive reflections about the value of the project. One artist wrote to the young people afterwards that she had learned a great deal from working with them and gained confidence herself. Memory was a theme, which resonated with the young people about their experiences.

"I learnt an awful lot from all of you and I will never forget it. I will also never forget you. I really liked cutting back the brambles around the seat because it made me remember doing that with my Grandma years ago. Thank you for all the memories"

"I enjoyed new experiences that I will remember for a long time"

"When I look back on our trips the sunset living sculpture first comes to mind and always will" (Lucazs Skapski *Via Lucem Continens*, 2000)

Several students, especially those who had experienced Chris Drury's Coppice Cloud Chamber in Phase 1 were upset to witness that it had been vandalised. Student evaluations a month later recorded that they remembered the weather, having *"fun times"* and two recalled Greg Pryor's 'Miracle of the Legs'. One other comment was the nice walk and *"the sound of the birds and feeling peaceful"*.

Two consecutive days May 2009

The group comprised a group of 21 children from the school with a wide age range from 5 up to 11 years old including some children from the HIU. This demanded deaf awareness from the team and was included in the training led by Mary Johncock, specialist teacher and consultant.

Each student was given a map (to follow the route and identify where each sculpture was located) and a sketchbook. They were encouraged to look at the planting of different trees, pattern, shapes, scale, fractals and repeat patterns.

The school felt that it would be good for the children especially those in the unit who experience difficulties in communicating verbally, giving them the opportunity to express themselves physically and artistically in order to convey some of their feelings. The other children were selected on the basis that they would also benefit and would support and mentor the other children.

The children's evaluations are made on film and in letters sent after the project. These reinforce the findings made with the other groups. Direct experience of the forest conjures a feeling of excitement as do the activities:
"Thank you for the lovely aventencher I like macking the sunpichers"

"Thank you so much for helping us making sculptures and I was exited to come and see bugs plants and even you, I rearly rearly rearly liked the bit where we made a sculptures out of chestnut trees, that was fun!"

"Well the forest is great because... there's loads of stuff to do" (DT film disc 1: 9.15).

Two students enjoy the experience of cutting coppice and using it to make sculpture:

Thank you comeing to the frorest with us. I like doing make with you. I like make a path and house. And we was cutting a brach."

Letter HIU primary: 'I like cutting the branches'

'I like looking at insects'

"thanck you for helping me with the trees like the bit wen we cat the chenut tree" (DT film disc 1: 7.16).

The children enjoy seeing the fauna:

"I saw some deer" (5.25)
"I think I saw a frog" (5.43)

"I lic look at isecx" (beautiful drawing of insects) child aged 5

as well as the sculptures:

"I liked all the sculptures as well" (DT film disc 1: 9.04).

"Thank you so much for showing us around the forest I loved every bit of it. The log house was amazing"

Asked about the favourite things *" When we were in that hut and the big bathtub"* (Chris Drury Cloud Chamber & Rosie Leventon's work 'Ring' (9.20)

The natural environment represents freedom as one child remarks enthusiastically to camera, spreading her arms: *"It's just nature, it's free space"* (DT film disc 1: 9.07) Another remarks: *"It felt really nice being out in the nature"* (9.32) To another child, the forest has a calming and soothing effect *" I wish I could come here again, it's really nice and quiet here not like the towns"* (DT film disc 1: 8.47). The same individual disclosed that there was some disruption at home and some uncertainty about the future, suggesting that the forest represented respite for her (researchers journal). The novelty of working with new people resurfaced: *"Meeting new people, building stuff"* (9.54) as well as the enjoyment of being inspired and working as a team: *"We've been having ideas off other people and we've done stuff ourselves. It was really fun"* (9.48).

One 5 year old was very keen on using the map to find sculptures and drew a map of the forest showing a good conceptual understanding of the space (researchers journal). Other children said they could not draw but used sticks to make marks on the forest floor instead, demonstrating how learning can be freed by outdoor space and that this kind of exploration can allow for experimentation and alternatives to conventional ideas of what constitutes drawing, as in this instance.

78

> ### Year 6 transition primary school group: Phase 2 only
>
> Three sessions March to July 2010
>
> 32 x Year 6 children in transition. Considered "young for their age" by the teacher.
>
> Worked with theme Sense of Place to complement school curriculum
>
> The theme of mapping was complemented by scientific survey using quadrats and identification exercises
>
> A final exhibition was held and a tree was planted in the school
>
> A sample session plan is included in Appendix 8

The children's exit evaluations show that the children most valued all aspects of making both in terms of enjoyment and their own learning. Many children mentioned tree identification as something they had learnt. This also featured in their memories of what they had done, with the SVA sculptures being identified both collectively and singly. The forest was also a theme, the trees and scale of it emerging as memorable as well as the atmosphere, which the children describe in their own language: " *it was big and cold and dark*" and " *it was dark and a bit light and also very cold*" then: *"the really tall trees all around dimming the light"*. One child remembered *"listening for the sounds"*. During the project itself one boy tells the researcher he prefers being outside to being in school and when asked why he says: *"I'm the sort of learner that does stuff – that's how I kind of learn"*(Disc 2 kinaesthetic 0.20-0.24).

Particular children greatly enjoyed the exercises in mapping and orientation and one child introduces the sculpture Superkingdom to the rest of the group as she has so fully engaged with this task (researchers journal). Another child finds a nightjar nest during the quadrat surveying task. These are extremely hard to spot but it turns out that this girl collects nests (Disc 2: nests: 0.8 – 0.14).

One group of children spot deer and are very excited by this (Disc 2 Eagles: 2.25 – 2.48). When they see great tits at Superkingdom and find a nest in one of the sculptures they are excited and this prompts speculation and empathy: " *they probably feel safe in there*" (researcher's journal). The audio material shows how the children ask lots of questions and initiate the idea to go and look at Jem Finer's sound sculpture.

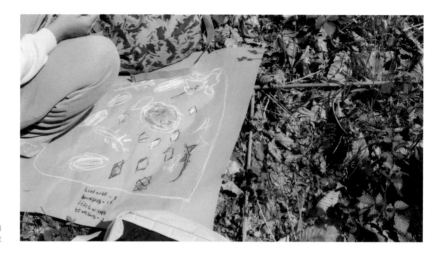

Quadrat exercise, drawing
and nightjar nest

Sun prints and evaluations
from final exhibition

INTERVIEWS

The remainder of this chapter will examine the interviews with teachers and practitioners to look for common themes in the findings concerning learning outcomes and experience of working with SVA. The table below shows the qualifications and experience of the interviewees who include a headteacher not involved with SVA and a deputy head involved in 'Down Time' Phase 2. A total of 8 individuals were interviewed in response to questionnaires.[49]

	Trained teacher	Artist	Forestry Ecology	CP practitioner	SVA practitioner	Years practice SVA	Down Time
FB	O	O			O	1.5	O
MB	O	O	O	O	O	11	
WG		O	O	O	O	1.5	O
SG	O					N/A	
PM	O					3	
JP	O					2	O
CR		O			O	5+	
LT		O			O	11	O

Fig. 3 Interviewees in terms of practice

In his interview, reflecting on three years of collaborative practice, PM discusses what are the educational outcomes from working with SVA and he says that these are broad, *"in history, geography, ecology, literacy, the physical stuff: the outcomes are vast"* (PM). Working with an SVA ecologist the children later identified a particular species of wasp back in their school grounds: *"nobody knew they were there"*. In addition PM points to learning and motor skills and making the connection between the chalk and charcoal and the landscape as learning outcomes. Discussing the value of being outdoors to children who are hyperactive, he says: *"you take them outside, automatically they calm down"*. He highlights the impact of the forest in terms of scale: *"they wouldn't see the playground as outdoors all the children we have brought to the forest they go wow it's the awe factor"*. Themes of mapping, orientation and cognitive ability also emerge in both primary school groups (Evaluations).

49 See Appendix 7 for more detail about interviewees

Questioned about the role that artists play, he also observes there is an issue of difference and contrast with the school environment: *"it's also that they can bring new ideas- not the constraints of the curriculum"*. He speaks about artists showing their own work and sketchbooks to the children who are impressed by their professional status. Commenting that *"the environment provokes a sense of freedom"* in young people in contrast to the constraints of the classroom, artist LT observes that the available materials can be more accessible, *"e.g drawing with sticks leaves on the forest floor is less daunting than a white piece of paper and a sharpened pencil"*. FB felt that the benefits of learning at SVA involved: *"an invaluable opportunity to learn without any distractions from their everyday surroundings"*. WG observes that working in school means that children are aware of what they should be doing which can: *"make it harder to break routines and change ways of doing things"* while in the forest *"they are naturally less constrained and able to think more creatively more quickly"* (WG).[50] Expanding on this theme MB, an outdoor learning specialist with CP, compares his practice with SVA and reflects: *"The main differences is the SVA work mostly takes place in the forest miles away from the school environment, the pupils walk into the day's work leaving behind school bells timetabled lessons and regulated break times. They manage their own needs and work in harmony with the weather, and physical stimulus the forest throws up. I've seen pupils work through horrendous rain just intent on creating their work, as well as those glorious light filled days in the outdoor workshop following dappled sun around the floor. Due to budget and a need for schools to spread their CP artist across the whole school time spent with whole classes and year groups dilutes the possible work, also the school space and politics dominate the pupils' experiences, they never seem to get fully away enough to experiment with space, place and time"*.

The idea of risk taking comes up in relation to particular children who will be more adventurous in the outdoor environment than they are in class: *"You allow more creativity more openness and more freedom perhaps it goes back to the risk taking they have limited materials they have no options but to take that risk and make the leap perhaps"* (PM). There is one girl in the class who took on a leadership role working in the forest but who *"keeps her head down in the classroom"* (PM). All five artists interviewed gave examples of this shift in learners of all ages when in the forest and of: *"seeing groups that were not expected to be very attentive doing the opposite"* (WG, also FB, CR, LT, MB). Of a special school, LT said: *"participants really benefited from using the tools and being able to interact with nature. Handling the insects and forest materials really worked well with the group"*. Such responses also led to: *"teachers being surprised at what individuals are capable of"* (CR).

50 See Horne Martin in Spencer and Blades 2006 p.92

The researcher remembers an instance where a boy produced a beautiful haiku poem and the teacher remarked that she could never get him to do any writing at all and that this would have greatly boosted his self esteem (Medhurst 2007 p.15). PM recalls another example: *"I know that the time we went to the burial mound – the amount of literacy we got out of them afterwards was incredible. Their imaginations were stimulated they came back and wrote all these mini legends and imagining all these reluctant writers. We had an exhibition in the hall and they displayed all their parchments. I don't think we would ever have got work of that quality out of that crew without the experience. I remember that on one of the visits they came out on a foggy morning and they were all telling each other ghost stories and that. They were covering their speaking and listening trying to scare each other it was cracking that morning it was eerie"* (PM).

In terms of unexpected outcomes another boy took on a leadership role in the forest in contrast with his performance in class. He showed maturity allowing his group to take the credit but was pleased with his achievement, although this may not have been lasting: *'It was certainly the case that he was more positive for a while"* (PM). Discussing another Year 6 group with a large number of boys, PM remembers how the project boosted their confidence:
"Like I say the one particular case the 20 boys who made a lasting impression there was a positive impact of those boys to see their own work in an exhibition in the school hall at the end and to share with parents and the whole school. Their self-esteem was really boosted for all those individuals".
Boys were cited by two artists as being likely to benefit from projects at SVA, as well as kinaesthetic learners and those who do not work well in a school environment (LT, CR and PM). MB felt that small groups had a better chance of being taken out of school. In Phase 2 one boy from the Year 6 group tells the researcher he prefers being outside to being in school because he is a kinaesthetic learner.[51]

The use of Leuven to support children in transition to secondary level as well as SEAL, which is used for younger children, was also the subject of one of the interview questions. PM felt that emotional literacy is strong in the school and had helped lead to high attainment targets. This had in turn meant that the LEA was keen to understand why the SATS results were so good and behavioural problems fewer, because for them this *"has to be quantifiable"*. Well-being was thought to be the factor. The school is considered an example of best practice but even so, their referrals are on the rise. This indicates that there are more children at risk of being excluded. PM sees a correlation between children who experience difficulties in their lives outside school and their inability to concentrate and be adventurous with their learning.

51 See p.78

The importance of connection with and developing empathy for the environment were also potentials of learning in a Land Art context that PM felt were significant. He felt that children are spending a lot of time with electronic media and are not taken out by their parents. The group's response to the damage to the Cloud Chamber was a case in point, as PM felt this might help: *"develop a thoughtful response to taking care of things in the environment"*. The perception that there are risks in the natural environment was also a factor although he felt that it was important for the children to experience some difficulty and discomfort in order to learn how to deal with these issues in life.

When questioned about the barriers to learning outside the classroom, major factors were felt to be funding, travel and the constraints on teachers imposed by the system (SG PM CR). In contrast with MB's observations above about coping with weather, LT observed that it could have a *"huge impact on learning within the forest"*. WG felt that there could be distractions in the forest perhaps preventing learning going into depth, while MB felt that the combination of art and ecology allowed *"learning in depth"* with particular features like the ant colonies *"creating an understanding of subtle ecologies and creating wonder"*. LT cited feelings of fear and insecurity in some participants and the vastness of the space, in contrast with positive associations of awe and wonder cited by PM.

The artistic process was thought to give students experience of problem-solving. *"Learning through art and the environment...can show how the different disciplines of learning come together and can be understood as part of a real living, working system...for many people the art allows a route through which to engage with more scientific or academic disciplines"* (WG) MB felt that the combination links *"stimuli from all aspects of a place, season, a world political view, a local view linking creative processes down the centuries"*. He also cited the *excellent documentation of the different sculptural responses to the forest"* giving *"SVA educators a depth to the presentation of the environment to...teachers and students"*. Emotional and personal learning skills were cited by LT, while FB felt that the challenges of working outdoors impacted positively and that the confidence gained by direct experience of the artistic process enabled participants to learn, better than they would in the classroom (also MB, CR, WG, LT).

CHAPTER FIVE

Conclusion

CONCLUSION

Apollinaire said
Come to the edge
It is too high
Come to the edge
We might fall
Come to the edge
And they came and they flew [52]

This dissertation has asked the question what is the value of experiential learning in a Land Art context and has sought to answer this through examination of primary research into SVA's project 'Down Time'. It has demonstrated a wide range of outcomes including knowledge and skill acquisition, enhanced geographical and environmental literacy, problem solving and decision making ability, affective knowledge, physical fitness, motor skill development, sensory stimulation and active play opportunities, social skills, sense of community, engaging with others, connectedness, lower ADHD, improved mental health and well-being, enhanced self-concept, spiritual enhancement, increased self esteem, personal and social development, environmental responsibility, positive values and attitudes, empathy and tolerance, risk assessment and resilience.[53] The recent Vibration Station project resulted in an overwhelmingly positive evaluation from the 72 students their teachers and families who were involved. Working with one Key Stage in Years 4 and 6 allowed very clear learning outcomes to be realised.[54] Sounds were recorded on Field trips to King's Wood and environments in Ashford and then edited back in the school. The students' work was displayed in an exhibition alongside that of artist Lee Patterson in the disused art college building in Ashford and many families came to visit. SVA's own body of research and practice continues to grow.

52 Helen O'Donoghue 'Come to the Edge' in Xanthoudaki et al. pp 85-86

53 Malone outcomes Appendix 7

54 Martin, 2010

There is a level of difficulty identified regarding this work contingent on funding, time, and the constraints and demands imposed by the system. In interviewing SG, the headteacher of an infant school with an interest in special needs and creativity, she identifies that this may be due to the view that *"creativity and free play (are) a stage that children go through and then it is over for them. This is constricting (and) leads to shallow understanding and I do feel that the education system still needs to use creativity as a tool for problem solving creativity and relationship building"*. In the same interview SG talks about a separation between education methodology and practice. She also asks:

"why do 98% of children cite playtime as their favourite thing? We can't ignore that and stop separating learning from fun". In this dissertation the evaluative material shows the beneficial effects of learning in the natural environment and in a real world context on so many levels, but pressures on schools may mean that LOTC has not resulted in a huge increase in outdoor activity in terms of lessons delivered outside or an increase in visits to cultural venues.[55]

That relationships underpin much of what all human culture is about is to revisit many themes of this paper. The positive findings and observations about value concerning SVA and its learning context pivot around notions of freedom and difference. Participants discover the freedom to renegotiate those relationships and to be freed from constraints and normative values. This can be very powerful and in particular for those cohorts who the system has failed to engage or who are deemed to have failed in the system. This is not to pretend that the answer lies in a formula, nor that this approach would work in every case. However, as bottom of the table for well-being for young people in the UNICEF study, it is clear that there is a problem here that urgently needs to be addressed.

During the writing of this dissertation, seismic shifts in government policy and funding have been taking place. The LOTC agenda, launched as a manifesto, rather than as an integrated part of the curriculum under the last government, is under threat. The old networks built with the local education authorities and delivery partners are being restructured and relationships are being lost as a result. Teachers see funding and transport as major barriers to accessing LOTC. However, SVA has established sound working relationships that do remain: these need to be consolidated and sustained. The challenge is how to communicate the value of experiential learning in a Land Art context to other partners in the mainstream. In a new era, the work with vulnerable groups and those at risk of exclusion and referral might prove to be the most viable for institutions with increasing pressures on their budgets. When other options narrow, headteachers and senior management teams

55 SG commented that she was aware of the LOTC manifesto *"more by luck than judgement"*

may be prepared to take a risk on what is still considered to be an alternative, experimental creative approach. Close working relationships will need to be in place, though for this to be considered. As SG notes, there are many schools who are unable to implement things on their own site, due to constraints, let alone engaging outside. As a keen advocate, but working in a deprived area, PM acknowledges that without the funding SVA provides, the school would not be able to visit. Malone concludes her paper by calling for a central clearing house for relevant research to make the case for LOTC to politicians: *"Without it the battle will continue to be between what is seen as core activities for children's education – the real work in the classroom and the additional 'fun' work that goes on outside"* (2008 p.25).

The gaps for future research may be to investigate themes such as cognitive mapping more deeply in the education programmes at SVA. This was trialled with Vibration Station to some extent, matching as it did the theme of sound mapping both geographically and imaginatively. Mapping was a popular activity particularly with primary school children in Phases 1 and 2 of 'Down Time' and geological maps have been used on other projects. The dissertation has also identified a need to find a way to communicate more closely to schools and policy makers what the outcomes are in a language that is easily translated. In spite of a wealth of qualitative material, it is still the mixed method approach that is better regarded by academics and educationalists. The FS system praised by Malone for its simplicity and replicability, could be further investigated by SVA and perhaps adapted for use as an evaluative tool in the education programmes. This would not replace our current practice, but should provide an effective framework to be used by artists, ecologists and teachers working in this context. It could be researched, adapted and trialled.

The necessity to work even more closely with partners has also been highlighted in the research. Without triangulation and peer dialogue, it is possible for practitioners to sit in their separate bunkers, fighting separate battles. The research is entirely dependent on the dedication and care shown by teachers, teaching assistants, care and social workers who can reflect on what happens in the space during these sessions and give them meaning based on their detailed knowledge of the children and young people taking part. Not least, the children and young people themselves demonstrate their willingness to participate and share. It is in this central space working with artists in the environment that experiences can be made, the curriculum or learning experience enhanced and relationships transformed. Dialogue allows the wider networks to collaborate and to understand one another better.

CPD could offer mutual benefits. Many gallery educators, artists and ecologists are not trained teachers. They could gain from learning about voice projection, especially when working in outdoor spaces. Developing opportunities for teachers, care and social workers and SVA teams to meet on a regular basis to engage in making could be a means of adding value to collaborations and to foster mutual respect and trust. Team building was a feature of Down Time that could be consolidated and extended. The use of film has also added enormous value to the research and it would be desirable to be able to fund a film maker as part of the team on all long term projects to help with creative evaluation. Film most powerfully and directly communicates the value of this learning to the outside world.[56] SVA should publish its education reports as an accompaniment to its artists' books and other publications. Materials could also be made available online to extend the reach of the research. Contact should be made with Malone about the central clearing space for this material.

For small organisations, small steps are best managed but integrity can be maintained and strength built through establishing links with bigger partners such as universities, to continue with research. At the same time it is important to take note of what Anna Cutler advocates and to be bold and ambitious. SVA wants to have some kind of eco-building in the forest, which could complement the education programmes and provide shelter when the weather threatens to undermine activities. It is a relatively modest aspiration but could also provide learning opportunities in itself.

"It is one of the marks of humanity and the only way to peace and the only way to co-existence in a fragile planet ecologically and in human terms, if we can develop the capacity to be able to allow other cultures find their space and within cultures, peoples' experience and stories" (Adams Falk and Dierking in Xanthoudaki et al p.88).

It is the art of with, as advocated in Leadbetter's paper:
Above all, and in the spirit of SVA's work:

"Learning with rather than learning from, should be the motto... going forward: learning through relationships not systems" (2008, p.70).

The researcher emerges from the labyrinth and with new journeys to make.

56 Feedback from NHS

Appendix 1
FIELD NOTES GUIDE

I am asking everyone involved in these projects to keep a reflective journal/ field notes of all the sessions we are planning with SVA this Summer.

Please note down all your observations about participants, remembered conversations, significant events as shared or noted by artists, teachers or care workers. I am reliant on the team for this information and the quality of the observations will have a direct bearing on the research outcomes. I will be asking you to share these materials with me over the course of the project.

Particularly relevant will be any changes noted over time.

DOWN TIME groups are all participants for whom a well-being agenda is particularly relevant. Equally there may be barriers to learning (see Maslow's Hierarchy of Needs http://www.businessballs.com/maslow.htm)

The following may indicate the themes the research will be exploring, but should not confine or limit your observations:

5 domains child development	Cognitive Physical Social Emotional Personal
Identity/orientation	Sense of self in relation to the environment or landscape: observations or remarks about forest, flora, fauna
Well-being	Emotional physical and mental Body language Confidence, self expression
Learning skills	Motor skills Observation Reflection Problem-based/real world Creative
Barriers	Personal aversions (to outdoors, dirt, bad weather) other access or travel personal or practical problems. Mistrust. Previous negative experiences or associations
Unexpected outcomes	Development in an area where previously none.

90

Appendix 2
MASLOW'S HIERARCHY OF NEEDS

Self-actualisation
personal growth and fulfilment

Esteem needs
achievement, status, responsibility, reputation

Belongingness and Love needs
family, affection, relationships, work group, etc

Safety needs
protection, security, order, law, limits, stability, etc

Biological and Physiological needs
basic life needs – air, food, drink, shelter, warmth, sex, sleep, etc

91

Appendix 3
HEIN EDUCATION THEORIES (p.25).

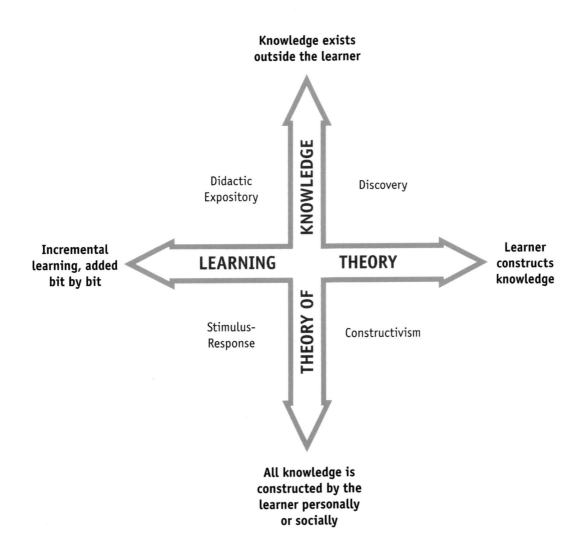

Reprinted from Hein, George. E., *Learning In The Museum*, 1988
with kind permission of Routledge publishers. Figure 2.4 page 25

92

Appendix 4
PRINGLE'S CGE MODEL (2006 p.38)

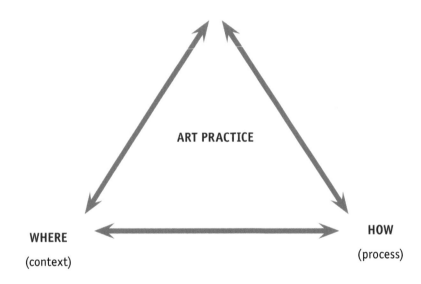

WHAT

(outcomes)

reflection   meaning   engagement

responsibility   empowerment

ART PRACTICE

WHERE

(context)

HOW

(process)

personal

socio-cultural

site specific

collaborating

analysing & reflecting

experimenting

engaging holistically

93

Appendix 5
Based on Cremin Barnes and Scoffham (2009)
Creative Teacher diagram p.10

THE CREATIVE TEACHER

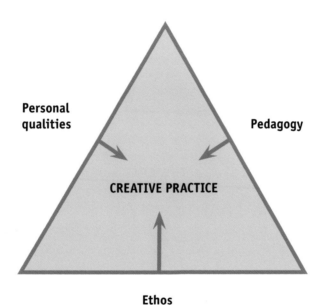

Personal qualities

Pedagogy

CREATIVE PRACTICE

Ethos

Based on Cremin Barnes and Scoffham (2009) Creative Teacher diagram p.10.
For further information please visit www.future-creative.org

Appendix 6
MALONE'S OUTCOMES OF EXPERIENTIAL LEARNING (2008 p.12)

OUTCOMES OF EXPERIENTIAL LEARNING LOTC		
Benefits	**Expression**	**Description**
Cognitive	What I Learn	Knowledge & Skill Acquisition
		Enhanced Environmental & Geographical Literacy
		Improved critical Skills & Thinking
		Better Decision Making & Problem Solving Ability
		Affective Knowledge
Physical	What I Experience	Physical fitness & Healthy Body
		Motor Skill Development & Fitness
		Balance Coordination
		Sensory Stimulation Active Play Opportunities
		Healthy Development & Nutrition
Social	How I Interact	Social Skills & Behaviours
		Sense of Community
		Engaging with Others
		Sociability
		Connectedness to Childs Inner & Outer Worlds
Emotional	How I Feel	Psychological Benefits, Lower ADHD
		Improved Mental Health & Well Being
		Enhanced Self-Concept
		Spiritual Enhancement
		Increased Self-Esteem
Personal	How I Respond	Personal & Social Development
		Environmental Behaviour Changes
		Environmental Responsibility
		Positive Values & Attitudes
		Empathy & Tolerance
		Risk Assessment & Resilience

Reproduced with the kind permission of Farm and Countryside Education

Appendix 7

INTERVIEWEES
FB – Trained art teacher with experience of secondary school and art school settings
Artist on Down Time Phases 1 & 2
Responded to questionnaire by email 18/8/10

MB – MB has a forestry, art and environmental background. Trained art teacher. An artist with a practice in ceramics and wood, and sculpture warden at SVA. Has worked with education and learning programme at SVA for 11 years and is a CP practitioner.
Responded to questionnaire by email 24/8/10

WG – artist and gardener also practitioner with CP
Artist on Down Time Phases 1 & 2
Responded to questionnaire by email 12/8/10

SG – Headteacher infant school Maidstone Kent: specialisms Early Years, Special Needs and Creativity
Interviewed Faversham, Kent 17/8/10

PM – deputy head and Year 6 teacher with primary involved in Down Time Phase 2 and other long term projects with SVA from 2007 – 2010
Interviewed SVA forest office 7/7/10

CR – artist and practitioner with CP. Worked with SVA 5 years +
Responded to questionnaire by email 12/8/10

LT – Photographer and experienced project manager.
Worked with SVA for 11 years
Project manager Down Time Phase 2
Responded to questionnaire by email 18/8/10

QUESTIONS FOR ALL ARTISTS
1. How long have you worked with SVA?

2. How does this compare with your work for Creative Partnerships? What are the similarities and what are the differences

3. What do you think are the benefits of learning in an outdoor Land Art context like SVA?

4. Do you think the work is particularly suited to certain groups? In your experience do certain groups respond more favourably than others?

5. Have you witnessed particular education benefits or outcomes (please give examples if possible)?

6. What are the barriers to learning in such a way/ in this context?

7. How do you feel that learning about the artistic process and through art combined with the environment can contribute to learning?

QUESTIONS FOR PM
1. You have worked with SVA for 3 years on a number of projects. Can you explain what you feel have been the education outcomes from working with an arts organisation also based in a forest environment?

2. What role do the following play in the projects?
a) outdoor environment
b) artists
c) art
d) ecology

3. How does it complement the curriculum (does it)?

4. What are the challenges involved in the work?

5. If there are children that SVA projects suit, what are the barriers and issues for other children and / teachers?

6. Can you comment on the instance in a Year 3 ? class where one boy apparently made a leap with his writing? This was observed by the teacher, who generously shared her observation and experience. How important is trust and building relationships in this work?

7. Do you use Leuven or SEAL? Can you explain what you regard as the role of well-being in learning/ education?

8. Using the Field Studies Guide, can you find examples, draw on observations or report on comments made by students or staff about project experiences?

QUESTIONS FOR SG
1. How long have you been teaching?

2. Do you have a specialist area?

3. Can you comment on creativity in schools? Do you think that SATS have any effect on creativity in school?

4. Is creativity included in curricula?

5. Are you aware of LOTC manifesto?

6. Does that use of the outdoors continue further up the school?

7. What place does culture have in Primary Education?

8. What are the barriers to LOTC?

9. How could SVA address the issue of engaging with schools

10. Do you think an SVA building would make a difference?

QUESTIONS FOR JP
1. How are young people referred to EKHNES?

2. Are there particular benefits that you think the project offers to your students? Are there education outcomes? If so, what are they?

3. What are the challenges?

4. Referring to the Field Notes Guide, can you identify any areas of the research that the project has addressed? Please use examples where possible.

5. What role do you think working directly with art and artists plays for your students and for the teaching team?

6. Do you think that novelty/difference plays a part? I mean by this both artists and outsiders who are not known and who don't know the students but also the context of the forest and the contemporary art sited there.

7. How much of a risk is it to take your students out of doors? Would you say that all staff feel confident with this? Do you have support from senior management?

8. EKHNES uses the Leuven scale for assessment. Can you say something about why this method was chosen (as opposed to or in addition to SEAL for example)?

9. Do you think that academic attainment is still considered as the most important assessment criteria for your students by the inspection and education authorities?

10. Are there observations or remarks made by your students or any changes you have noticed that might be attributed to participation in Down Time?

APPENDIX 8
SAMPLE SESSION PLAN

Year 6 PROJECT – 25th May 2010 Yr 6: 32 children
Meet car park 9.30: Artists LT and WG + researcher
Walk begins: Intro & General health and safety talk in car park
Leave from car park 15.00 (total visit time 5 hrs 30 mins)

Theme: Senses of Place

Timing	Location	Activity
10.00	Meadow Area	Where are we? Google map copy to compare with SVA map(Peter to prepare before forest) Kent, AONB Downs What is a forest? Why are forests important to the environment? What happens here? Who works here? Coppicing and forestry and SVA. Animals and habitats
10.30 –10.45	Richard Harris Untitled (Living Arch) 1994	What is this piece made of? How is the landscape around it? How is place important to artists How will it change through time Drawing exercise – shape and form
10.45 – 11.10	On the path to the outdoor studio stop at three areas: 1 Tall sweet chestnut area on the right of path. 2. Dense pine tree area 3. Beech area within outdoor studio	Change of tree species from chestnut to pine and beech. How does each area feel? How does it sound? – one minute listening exercise within each area, compare.
11.15	Via ant hill	Discuss habitats and forest dwellers. Bluebell acid test using ant nest – discuss defence mechanism.
11.30 – 11.45	London Fieldworks Superkingdom 2008	New animal habitats modelled on grand palaces of leaders Mussolini, Stalin and Ceaucescu. Can we see any animals living there? Any nests? What animals might live here? Drawing exercise.

11.45 – 12.10	On the ride	Joint long drawing exercise - mapping
12.10 – 12.20	Rosie Leventon Ring 2003 An artist interested in archaeology Inspired by the ancient barrows in the forest	What shape is this piece? Tell them deer drink at the pool Can you see any footprints? What is reflected in the pool? In Spring the bluebells will come up all round the ring
12.30 – 1.00	Outdoor Studio	Lunch
1.00 – 1.10	Outdoor Studio	Will to introduce afternoon creating session. Health & Safety tool talk.
1.10 – 2.30	Outdoor Studio	3D Map – create a route using found materials. Create sculptures/creatures at different sections on map. Relate to theme of PLACE.
2.30 – 2.45	Outdoor Studio	Review work created. Discuss next session
2.45	Pack up	To be at car park for 3pm

Next session:

Visit to B52 sculpture – Discuss scale and viewpoint
Walk different route through to the burial mound and pond.

Exercise:
'Patterns and processes' Key stage 2 curriculum
Looking at scale discuss the patchwork of the whole forest whilst also using quadrants to look at patterns in the forest floor. Using 10m x 10m quadrants and 1m x 1m quadrants. Complete surveys in different areas of the forest: meadow, conifers, chestnut etc. This exercise would encourage identification, drawing and measuring. Small sketchbooks would be given out to allow for drawing and write up of results etc.

DISSERTATION BIBLIOGRAPHY

ACE December 2009. *Beyond Their Walls*
http://www.artscouncil.org.uk/publication_archive/beyond-their-walls/
Accessed 25/1/2010

ACE April 2008. *New Landscapes: Outdoor arts development plan* available
at:http://www.artscouncil.org.uk/publication_archive/new-landscapes-
outdoor-arts-development-plan/ Accessed 25/1/2010

Austin, R. ed. 2007. *Letting the Outside In: developing teaching and
learning beyond the early years classroom* Trentham Books

Barlow, N. ed. 1958. *The autobiography of Charles Darwin 1809-1882. With
the original omissions restored. Edited and with appendix and notes by his
grand-daughter Nora Barlow.* F1497 available at: http://darwinonline.org.
uk/recollections.html accessed 14/7/10

Beard, C & Wilson, J.P., 2002. *Experiential Learning: a best practice
handbook for educators and trainers* Kogan Page Ltd

Bell, S., Ward Thompson, C. and Travlou, P. 2003.
*Contested views of freedom and control: children, teenagers and urban
fringe woodlands in Central Scotland.* Urban Forestry and Urban Greening2,
pp.87–100.

Bentley, T. *Learning Beyond the Classroom* 1998 Routledge

Bigge, M & Shermis, S. 2004. 6th edition *Learning Theories for Teachers*
Allyn and Bacon

Boud, D. Keogh, R. & Walker, D., eds 1985 *Reflection: Turning Experience
into Learning.* Routledge

Brice-Heath, S. and Wolf, S. *Visual Learning in the Community School* 2004
Creative Partnerships: *Art is all about Looking* 2004a *Hoping for Accidents*
2004b *Sharing a Common Vision: community learning for community
futures* 2004c available at: http://www.creativitycultureeducation.org/
data/files/vlc-sharing-a-common-vision-2004-121.pdf accessed 21/7/10

Brookes, A. (2004). Astride a long-dead horse. Mainstream outdoor
education theory and the central curriculum problem. *Australian Journal
of Outdoor Education*, 8(2), pp.22-33.

Brookes, A. (2003). A critique of neo-Hahnian outdoor education theory. Part one: challenges to the concept of 'character building'. *Journal of Adventure Education and Outdoor Learning*, 3(1), pp.49-62.

Brookes, A. (2003). A critique of neo-Hahnian outdoor education theory. Part two: 'the fundamental attribution error' in contemporary outdoor education discourse. *Journal of Adventure Education and Outdoor Learning*, 3(2), pp.119-132.

Brown, P. & Mills, D. (2004) *Art and Wellbeing* Australia Council available at: http://www.australiacouncil.gov.au/research/community_arts/ reports_and_publications/art_and_wellbeing2 accessed 14/6/09

Burgin, V. 1996. *In/Different Spaces Place and Memory in Visual Culture* University of California Press

Canter, D. 1977. *The Psychology of Place* The Architectural Press Ltd

Carlson, A. 2002. 2nd edition., *Aesthetics and the Environment* Routledge

Ceppi, G. & Zini, M.1998. *Children Spaces Relations* Reggio Children and Comune di Reggio Emilia

Chances4Change website http://www.wellbeingsoutheast.co.uk/ chances4change/

Chawla, L. 1999. 'Life paths into effective environmental action', *Journal of Environmental Education,* 31, 15. Requested University of Sussex library March 2010

Chawla, L. and Cushing, D.F., 2007. *'Education for strategic environmental behavior'*, *Environmental Education Research,* 13, 437 - 452.

Clayton, S. & Opotow, S. eds., 2003. *Identity and the Natural Environment: The Psychological Significance of Nature* MIT Press

Cremin,T. Barnes,J. and Scoffham, S. 2009. *Creative Teaching for Tomorrow – Fostering a Creative State of Mind* Future Creative CIC

Croxford, L. Ducklin, A. Frame, B. Tinklin, T., 2001. *Gender and pupil performance* Interchange 70, Issue 31 University of Edinburgh Practical Research for Education website available at: http://www.pre-online.co.uk/pre_feature_articles.asp accessed 12/2/10

103

Cutler, A. 2010. *What Is To Be Done, Sandra? Learning in Cultural Institutions of the Twenty-First Century* Tate Papers issue 13 available at http://www.tate.org.uk/research/tateresearch/ tatepapers/10spring/cutler.shtm accessed 1/7/10

Dewey, J. 1997. (first published 1938)., *Experience and Education* Simon and Schuster

Drew, S. and Kent, L. 2005. *King's Wood – A Context* Stour Valley Arts

Ellis-Smith, G., 2003. *Ancient Land - Current Connections* http://wilderdom.com/html/Ellis-Smith2003AncientLandCurrentConnect ions.htm accessed 25/1/2010

Enwright, C., 2010. *Links between Developmental Trauma (Complex Trauma), Brain Development, Attachment and Behaviour* Training Notes Kid's Company Unpublished

Ernst, J, and Monroe, M., 2006. 'The effects of environment-based education on students: critical thinking skills and disposition toward critical thinking." *Environmental Education Research,* 12, pp.429 - 443. Accessed 16/2/10

Fjortoft, I, and Sageie., J. 2000. 'The Natural environment as a playground for children: landscape description and analyses of a natural landscape', *Landscape and Urban Planning,* 48, pp.83-97.

Fleming, M. 2nd edition 2010 *Arts in Education and Creativity: a literature review* Creativity Culture and Education available at: http://www. creativitycultureeducation.org/research-impact/literature-reviews/ accessed 31/5/10

Freire, P. 1996. 3rd edition., *Pedagogy of the Oppressed* Penguin Books

Garraud, C. 2007. *L'Artiste Contemporain et La Nature* Editions Hazan

Galton, M. 2008. *Creative Practitioners in schools and classrooms Final report of the project: The Pedagogy of Creative Practitioners in Schools* Faculty of Education, University of Cambridge Available at http://www. creativitycultureeducation.org/research-impact/thematic-research/ Accessed 5/2/10

104

Goleman, D. 1996. *Emotional Intelligence* Bloomsbury

Grant, B & Harris, P. 1991.*The Grizedale Experience*1991 Canongate Press

Grizedale Arts http://www.grizedale.org/about/

Gustavson, P., 2001. *Meanings of Place: Everyday Experience and Theoretical Conceptualisations* in Journal of Environmental Psychology 21 pp5-16.

Harvard Papers 2004., *Children's Emotional Development Is Built into the Architecture of their Brains* Working Paper 2 National Scientific Council on the Developing Child
Available at: http://developingchild.harvard.edu/library/reports_and_working_papers/working_papers/wp2/ Accessed 18/3/10

Harvard Papers 2004.,*Young Children Develop in an Environment of Relationships* National Scientific Council on the Developing Child
Available at: http://developingchild.harvard.edu/index.php/library/reports_and_working_papers/working_papers/wp1/ Accessed 18/3/10

Hein, G., 1991. Constructivist learning theory. Institute for Inquiry.
Available at: /http://www.exploratorium.edu/ifi/ resources/constructivistlearning.html (accessed 18/3/10)

Hein, G.E. 1998. *Learning in the Museum* Routledge

Holt, J. 1982. 15th edition *How Children Fail* Pelican Books

Jess, P. Massey, D. eds., 1995. *A Place in the World* Open University

Kastner, J. & Wallis, B. 1998. *Land and Environmental Art* Phaidon

Keeton, M.T. 1976. *Experiential Learning* Jossey Bass

Kiwon, M. 2004 2nd ed., *One Place After Another: Site-Specific Art and Locational Identity* Cambridge Massachusetts

Kolb, D.A. 1984. *Experiential Learning: Experience as the Source of Learning and Development* Prentice Hall

Laevers, F. Spring 2000 , *Deep-level-learning and the Experiential Approach in Early Childhood and Primary Education* Early Years, Volume Issue 20 (2) pp. 20 - 29

Laevers, F & Moons, J. 1997 *Making Care and Education more effective through wellbeing and involvement. An introduction to Experiential Education* available at: http://www.richmond.gov.uk/experiential_education.pdf

Laevers, F. interview http://www.ltscotland.org.uk/mp4/SLF/FerreLaeversInterview.mp4
experiential education http://education.wiltshire.gov.uk/html/early_years.html

The Leuven system: http://www.kent-eps.org.uk/lpsa2/summary.pdf

Leadbetter, C. 2008 *What's Next? 21 Ideas for 21st Century Learning* The Innovation Unit available at: http://www.innovationunit.org/about-us/publications/whats-next.html accessed 14/6/10

Learning Theories available at: http://www.learning-theories.com/ accessed 23/3/10

Leuven assessment model http://www.kent-eps.org.uk/lpsa2/summary.pdf

Lofland L. and Lofland J. 1995 *Analysing Social Settings* 3rd edition Wadsworth Publishing Co

Louv, R. 2008. 2nd edition., *Last Child in the Woods* Algonquin books

Martin, L. 2010. *Vibration Station report* Stour Valley Arts unpublished

Malone, K. 2008. *Every Experience Matters: an Evidence Based Research Report on the Role of Learning Outside the Classroom for Children's Whole Development from Birth to Eighteen Years.* Stoneleigh Park: FACE Available:http://www.faceonline.org.uk/index.php?Itemid=850&id=1308&option=com_content&task=view accessed 15/2/10

Maslow's Hierarchy of Needs available at: http://www.businessballs.com/maslow.htm accessed 6/4/10

Medhurst, L. 2007. *Cluster Project Report Stour Valley Arts* unpublished

Medhurst, L. January 2009. *Ecologies of Practice Outdoor Learning and the Arts* MA Short term paper University of Sussex

Moon, J. 2004. *A Handbook of Reflective and Experiential Learning* Routledge Falmer

106

Munoz, F. Bogner, F. Clement, P. Graça, S. Carvalho, C., 2009.
Teachers' conceptions of nature and environment in 16 countries
Journal of Environmental Psychology 29 pp.407-413

National Institute of Adult Continuing Education (NIACE) 2009 Lifelong
Learning and the Early Years Margaret Lochrie IFLL SEctor Paper 3
avaiable at http://www.niace.org.uk/lifelonglearninginquiry/docs/IFLL-
Sector-Paper3.pdf

Neuroscience interviews UCL Wellcome Trust
http://www.ucl.ac.uk/histmed/audio/neuroscience accessed 16/5/10

O'Brien, L, and Murray, R. 2006. *A Marvellous Opportunity for Children to
Learn: A Participatory Evaluation of Forest School in England and Wales.*
Surrey: Forestry Commission England, Forest Research.

Ofsted 2003. *Boys' achievement in secondary schools* available at http://
www.ofsted.gov.uk/Ofsted-home/Publications-and-research/Browse-
all-by/Education/Pupils/Boys-achievement-in-secondary-schools/
(language)/eng-GB accessed 16/2/10

Ofsted 2003. *Yes he can – schools where boys write well* available at http://
www.ofsted.gov.uk/Ofsted-home/Forms-and-guidance/Browse-all-by/
Other/General/Yes-he-can-Schools-where-boys-write-well/(language)/
eng-GB accessed 16/2/10

O'Neill, C. 2006 *Mapping Lives Exploring Futures* Irish Museum of Modern Art

Pringle, E. 2006 *Learning in the Gallery: Context, Process, Outcomes.* engage

Pringle, E. 2009 The Artist as Educator: Examining Relationships
between Art Practice and Pedagogy in the Gallery Context Tate Papers
Issue 11, available at:
http://www.tate.org.uk/research/tateresearch/tatepapers/09spring/
emily-pringle.shtm accessed 21/7/10

Pringle, E. (2008) *Artists' Perspectives on art practice and pedagogy*, in
Creative Learning Arts Council England 2008 Edited by Sefton Green, J.
available at: http://www.creative-partnerships.com/data/files/creative-
learning-booklet-26.pdf accessed 21/7/10

Raney, K. 2008. Editorial: Art and Climate Change in *engage 21: Art and
Climate Change.* engage

Richard Long http://www.richardlong.org/ accessed 16/5/10

107

Robinson, K. 2001. *Out of Our Minds* Capstone

Read, H. 1947 6th edition., *Education Through Art* Faber and Faber

SATS test boycott available at: http://news.bbc.co.uk/1/hi/
education/8635017.stm accessed 22/4/10

Sanders, D. Duemler J. and Hartman E., December 2009 *Nature of
experience: engaging special needs learners through the natural world* in
NFER practical research for education issue 42 pp. 56–63 available at:
http://www.pre-online.co.uk/index.asp accessed 12/2/10

Sekules, V. Tickle, L. & Xanthoudaki, M., 2003. *Researching Visual Arts
Education in Museums and Galleries* Kluwer Academic Publishers

Social and Emotional Aspects of Learning) SEAL curriculum available at
(http://nationalstrategies.standards.dcsf.gov.uk/primary/publications/
banda/seal) accessed 3/5/10

Spencer, C. and Blades, M. eds., 2008. 2nd ed. *Children and Their
Environments* Cambridge University Press

Taylor, B. ed. 2008. *Inspiring Learning in Galleries 02: Research Reports.*
engage

Thistlewood, D 1994. *Herbert Read* PROSPECTS: the quarterly review
of comparative education (Paris, UNESCO: International Bureau of
Education), vol. 24, no.1/2, pp. 375–90 UNESCO: International Bureau
of Education,
available at:http://www.ibe.unesco.org/publications/ThinkersPdf/reade.
pdf accessed 2/5/10

Turton, D. *Meaning of Place in a World of Movement*
http://www.rsc.ox.ac.uk/PDFs/workingpaper18.pdf accessed 9/2/10

Velardea, D Fryb G, Tveitb M., 2007. *Health effects of viewing landscapes –
Landscape types in environmental psychology* in Urban Forestry & Urban
Greening 6 pp.199–212

Vygotsky's Social Development Theory available at: http://www.learning-
theories.com/vygotskys-social-learning-theory.html accessed 15/4/10

Whitaker, P. 1995. *Managing to Learn: Aspects of Reflective and
Experiential Learning in Schools* Cassell

Thanks are due to a great many people who have contributed to this research and formed part of the community of learning that was and is Down Time. Without the generosity of the artists, film makers, teachers, care and social workers, SVA colleagues and all the children and young people who have been and continue to be involved with Stour Valley Arts, this book would not have been possible. I hope that it will help to promote the value of outdoor learning and in particular to celebrate the unique context of King's Wood, Challock, Kent.

Lucy Medhurst
April 2011

Published in 2012 by Stour Valley Arts
Stour Valley Arts
King's Wood Forest Office
Challock
Kent TN25 4AR
www.stourvalleyarts.org.uk

ISBN: 978-0-9558719-4-8

Distributed by Cornerhouse Publications
70 Oxford Street, Manchester M1 5NH
t: +44 (0)161 200 1503
e: publications@cornerhouse.org

Text © Lucy Medhurst
Film © Hope Fitzgerald,
Photography © Hope Fitzgerald,
Laura Thomas and Lucy Medhurst

British Library Cataloguing In Publication Data. A catalogue record of this book is available from the British Library.

Design: loupdesign.co.uk

STOURVALLEYARTS

chances4change
Improving health and well-being
for people in South East England